HOLD FIRM

Francis Xavier Carty

Hold Firm
JOHN CHARLES MCQUAID
AND THE SECOND VATICAN COUNCIL

the columba press

First published in 2007 by
the columba press
55A Spruce Avenue, Stillorgan Industrial Park,
Blackrock, Co Dublin

Cover by Bill Bolger
Origination by The Columba Press
Printed in Ireland by ColourBooks Ltd, Dublin

ISBN 978 1 85607 585 5

Table of Contents

To that eminent churchman
now deceased
who said

'I thank you for what you are doing.
There is a great need for this work.'

And to the many people – publishers, interviewees, archivists,
supervisers, examiners, public relations colleagues, family,
friends and utter strangers who have been so helpful

Thanks to the principal sources of the research:

DDA: Dublin Diocesan Archives, Archbishop's House, Drumcondra
NAI: National Archives of Ireland, Bishop Street
UCD: James Joyce Library, University College Dublin, Belfield
John Paul II Library, St Patrick's College/National University of Ireland, Maynooth
DIT: Dublin Institute of Technology Library, Aungier Street
National Library of Ireland, Kildare Street
Central Catholic Library, Merrion Square

Very Rev John Patrick Canon Battelle
John Brophy
Gay Byrne
Rev Thomas Butler, SM
His Eminence Desmond Cardinal Connell, emeritus Archbishop of Dublin
Rt Rev Mgr Patrick J. Corish
Rt Rev Mgr Jerome Curtin
Rev Sean Fagan, SM
Rt Rev Mgr G. Thomas Fehily
The late Joseph Fitz-Patrick
Rev Austin Flannery, OP
Joseph F. Foyle
Vincent B. Gallagher
Very Rev J. Anthony Gaughan
Michael H.Gill
The late Seamus Grace
The late Mgr Stephen Greene
The late Rev Eltin Griffin, O.Carm
John Horgan
Rev Michael Hurley, SJ
The late Venerable Archdeacon Patrick Leahy
Ann Lee
Rev Aidan P. Lehane, CSSp
Elizabeth Lovatt-Dolan
Rev Dermod McCarthy
Rt Rev Mgr James Ardle Canon MacMahon
The late Seán Mac Réamoinn
Louis McRedmond
Maeve McRedmond
Patrick Masterson
Most Rev Donal Murray, Bishop of Limerick
The late Joseph F.Power
David Rice
David C. Sheehy

HOLD FIRM

Rt Rev Mgr Thomas Stack
Rt Rev Mgr Owen Canon Sweeney
Rt Rev Mgr Conor K. Ward

And others, some of whom wish to remain anonymous.

Introduction

On 25 January 1959, ninety days after his election, Blessed John XXIII, the 77-year-old Pope, made the completely unexpected announcement of his plan to convoke the Twenty-First Ecumenical Council, the first since Vatican I in 1869-1870. He hoped it would promote closer unity between the Roman Catholic Church, the Orthodox Christian churches which split from Rome in the eleventh century and the other Christian churches which emerged from the sixteenth century Protestant Reformation. In the immediate term, he saw it as an attempt by the church to update itself, insofar as that would be found necessary, in interpretation and presentation of its doctrines, its liturgical and devotional ceremonial, disciplinary practices and its administration. The Italian word *aggiornamento* (updating) came to symbolise much of the Pope's thinking on the Council and he referred to it often as an opening of the windows in the Vatican to let in some fresh air. He was anxious that it would lead the church to engage more positively with the modern world, as it had displayed an attitude of defence – even a siege mentality – and of reaction and suspicion to what was new in the world since the trauma of the Reformation and the Council of Trent (1545-1563).

The Council was attended by almost all of the 2,500 Catholic bishops, with certain dignitaries and invited observers from other churches. It held four sessions in Rome in the autumns of 1962, 1963, 1964 and 1965. Blessed John XXIII died in June 1963 and his successor, Pope Paul VI, saw the Council to its conclusion. It examined a succession of doctrinal, liturgical, social and other issues confronting the church, often in an animated and even contentious manner, in closed sessions which were conducted entirely in the Latin language. However, its deliberations did not remain secret and, by the later sessions, the world knew, soon after each meeting, exactly who had said what. There resulted sixteen documents on topics ranging from The Church, Liturgy, Ecumenism, Priestly Formation, Missions and Religious Freedom to the Church in the Modern World. These documents were voted upon and passed by the bishops and signed by the Pope to become official Catholic Church teaching. Subsequently, directives for their implementation were issued by the Roman Curia (the Vatican Civil Service) and implemented, through national hierarchies, by the bishops in their dioceses. The momentum of change created by the Council and the documents was such that many more changes came that were not specifically included in the documents, but seen as part of the spirit and intention of the Council.

Archbishop John Charles McQuaid

John Charles McQuaid (1895-1973) was Archbishop of Dublin from 1940 to 1972. He was theologically conservative and retained an authoritarian style of management and attitude towards the office of bishop that was still common then and generally accepted at all levels in society.

Dublin's archbishops, since the twelfth century, have tended to adopt strong and often individual positions. Their ecclesiastical primacy has not always been recognised, but their proximity to the seat of political power, and Dublin's position as the most populous diocese, has given them a *de facto* dominance. Archbishop McQuaid was chosen into this tradition, not from the priests of the diocese, but from a religious congregation, the Holy Ghost Fathers, where he had been President of Blackrock College secondary school for boys. He remained one of the most prominent, and controversial, Irish churchmen of the twentieth century, often influencing government policy and national thinking, contributing to the drafting of the Irish Constitution in 1937 and being a central figure in the clash with Dr Noël

Browne, Minister for Health, over a Mother and Child medical scheme in 1951, which led to the fall of the government.

The changing Ireland of the 1960s

In 1959, Éamon de Valera was succeeded as Taoiseach (Prime Minister) by Seán Lemass, bringing to an end the era that started with the Easter Rising of 1916. There were major changes in government policy and Ireland's relationship with the world. The new government strategy was to encourage overseas industry with generous grant-aid. This led to job creation, a reversal of the emigration trend after more than a hundred years and a new prosperity. The inauguration of the national television station, Telefís Éireann, on 31 December 1961, was a catalyst for debate and the broadening of views, opinions, attitudes and values. Free secondary education was introduced in 1967, leading to a major expansion in secondary and third level education. Through the 1960s Ireland moved along the path to the European Economic Community and became a full member on 1 January 1973. Violence in Northern Ireland eased in the early 1960s but arose again from 1968 in response to the civil rights issue, the emergence of the Provisional IRA and similar paramilitary groups on the unionist side. In 1972 the article in *Bunreacht na hÉireann* (*The Constitution of Ireland*), that recognised the 'special position' of the Catholic Church, was removed by referendum.

The scope of this book

This book originated in a doctoral thesis which examined how Archbishop McQuaid handled the Vatican Council and its aftermath in his diocese and whether this influenced his relationships with his diocesan priests and laity up to his retirement in 1972. Interviews were conducted with priests and laity who were in the Dublin diocese during the 1960s, followed by examination of the McQuaid papers in the Dublin Diocesan Archives, which were opened on a phased basis from 1998. Other archival and relevant secondary sources were also consulted.

Processes and outcomes of the theological debates engendered by the Second Vatican Council are indicated, but it is not within the scope of this book to adjudicate on the theological issues, nor to resolve disagreement on them, nor to determine the correctness of John Charles McQuaid's own theological positions. The implementation of the Council's decisions was still ongoing when he retired in 1972.

One issue, which preceded the Council and then became its by-product, was the church's ban on artificial contraception. Pope Paul VI withdrew the topic from consideration at the Council and, in 1968, retained the ban in an encyclical letter, *Humanae Vitae*. The linkage of this issue with the Council, and its impact in McQuaid's final years, are the reasons for including it here.

McQuaid's handling of certain issues which have been topical recently, such as child sex abuse, child adoption, conditions in orphanages, industrial schools (reformatories) or convent-run laundries, are not considered here. Such examination would take the focus away from the Council and stretch the timescale of the research back to earlier years of McQuaid's episcopacy. Some interviewees raised aspects of these issues but their evidence was not of sufficient strength to draw conclusions.

This is not a study of Catholic Church power and influence in Irish politics and society, which were given a firm anchor in the era of Paul Cardinal Cullen, Archbishop of Dublin (1852-1878), and continued to the 1950s. Many scholarly works have established the evidence of this power and influence, which McQuaid used to the full. Nor is this a biography of John Charles McQuaid. An extended essay by John Feeney (1974) attempted an assessment and a full-length work by John Cooney (1999) was informative, well-researched and attracted considerable controversy. Feeney (who died in an air crash in 1985) was a student activist and journalist in the 1960s and Cooney has been a prominent journalist and writer in Dublin since the early 1970s.

Several of the interviewees are among the small number of survivors from McQuaid's circle of friends and some of them are on record here for the first time with their memories and interpretations of what they witnessed. Also, the archives have re-vealed interesting and relevant documents and letters that have not been used in previously published work.

The Dublin Diocesan Archives contain some 700 boxes on Archbishop McQuaid alone, but they can be frustrating because there were not photocopiers until the final few years, and earlier letters were carbon-copied or re-written by hand and preserved only if important for subsequent reference to decisions taken or precedents created. One has to wonder, apart from thousands of telephone calls, what McQuaid wrote in many untraced letters to provoke the comments and responses that are often in the replies. The Fr Roland Burke Savage letters, for example, are il-luminating. In many cases, however, we have the comments which McQuaid wrote on letters received, sometimes as points for reply but very often just his first thoughts and memory aids for his own reference.

CHAPTER ONE

The Enigma of John Charles McQuaid

Archbishop John Charles McQuaid of Dublin, more than thirty years after his death, remains as much of an enigma as he was during his long tenure in Ireland's largest diocese, which by 1972 numbered more than 800,000 Catholics. Mention him still to those of his time and many will insist on their undying love and reverence for him, while others will not listen to a good word. Everybody seems to have a strong opinion, whether based on close acquaintance or on hearsay and anecdote, about a man whom many rarely or never met.

Young people of today, in a world of greater informality and openness of expression, cannot understand the aura that seemed to radiate from the 'palace' in Drumcondra. It often created the image of a stern, severe, forbidding man, a killjoy, who personified the Catholic Church in Dublin. He was imagined to be everywhere and to know about everything and everybody. There was a palpable anxiety, and often a fear of rebuke from an archbishop who might not approve of this, or of that. There were a few in his closer acquaintance who liked to let it be known that they had the inside opinion even on questions and matters of which he was unaware.

Whatever his critics might say, the evidence is overwhelming that he was an outstanding administrator and a man of strategic vision who anticipated issues long before most other people. He was dedicated to his work as archbishop, never off-duty, a man who showed an unfailing concern for the sick, the poor and the under-privileged, but combined this with a grandiose, sometimes renaissance-like courtly style, and the authoritarian approach to management that was usual at the time, with a rigid insistence on discipline and obedience, especially in small matters. Even close friends admit that he was very strict, and exact, and fussy about detail.

Fr Tom Butler, a Marist priest and school headmaster, who had frequent dealings with him, sums up Archbishop McQuaid's consciousness of his role and duty as bishop:

> His mentality was that 'I am the Pope's man here in Ireland, here in this big archdiocese of Dublin, I am the guardian of the Faith, I am the custodian of the Covenant. I am the teacher of faith and morals' and I think that was a grave responsibility and it weighed heavily on him.

This conviction led to a rigorous defence of what he regarded as the rights of the church in all spheres of public and private life. Mgr Stephen Greene sees this as 'paramount' in his thinking: '... there is no doubt about that ... he would not have changed ... He would have been a force to be reckoned with'. This also led to the contrast between the very humble man and what Mgr Tom Stack describes as the 'theatricality' of the public display of his office. Mgr Stack points to the Irish tradition of 'church ascendancy' which peaked in the years before Vatican II when the church 'triumphant' was dominant: '... everybody was in awe of the bishop, people kissed his ring and he wore all the paraphernalia and cloaks.' This was all many people saw of John Charles, either at ceremonies or through photographs in the newspapers. Some saw it as ridiculous and overdone, but it appealed to others. One retired parish priest remembers

> one woman, who liked him, saying: 'What I love about him is he is so churchy.' And it struck me that's a good description because if you met him you didn't feel you were meeting a man, you felt you were meeting a church. You felt you were impressed by him.

Derek Scott recalls McQuaid's visits to the Holy Ghost Club for Boys, Dún Laoghaire:

> It was a great state occasion. He would be driven up in his huge car. He was always attired as an archbishop of the time should be and escorted by various minions. And you met him at the door and you kissed his ring and you did all the usual things. And he arrived spot on time.

Mgr Ardle MacMahon, his secretary, sees it as a style of leadership, the 'mystique approach', as exercised by people like General de Gaulle and not the populist approach of, say Blessed John XXIII, which shares with everybody. Desmond Cardinal Connell, emeritus Archbishop of Dublin, often got the impression that John Charles would have looked to Pope Pius XII as the model, and 'Pius XII did give that impression of the supreme monarch.' Others, however, mention Pope Pius XI as a closer model.

McQuaid saw his strong predecessor, Paul Cardinal Cullen (1852-78), as a model, describing him as 'silent, magnanimous, farseeing' and 'as heedless of self-justification after death, as he was intrepid in administration during life'.[1] David Sheehy, Dublin diocesan archivist, recognises this parallel with Cullen in McQuaid's austere public image, 'impervious or indifferent to criticism and needless of justification'.[2]

In 1933, Archbishop McQuaid preached at the episcopal consecration of Joseph Byrne CSSp, saying the bishop 'has for task to keep his [Christ's] spouse, the church, inviolate, by the stainless orthodoxy of his teaching' and that:

> He is the fount of spiritual power in his diocese ... the father of the children of the church, who are born to God in baptism ... the church shall ever have for ordinary rulers, bishops.[3]

McQuaid was diligent and constant in his duties, and Vincent Gallagher, a pupil in Blackrock College during the McQuaid years, and later a leading church architect, confirms that he 'would reply to everything himself, personally ... and rapidly, in writing'. Ann Lee, the first female member of staff at Archbishop's House, says he preferred to take short breaks rather than long holidays and these breaks were often in Rockwell College in Co Tipperary. He described them to the college president, Fr Aidan Lehane, as 'a few days' withdrawal'.

While he was very much conscious of his position as ruler of the church in his diocese, he was probably ahead of some of his contemporaries in his belief that the church should not be solely 'clerical'. He told his Public Image Committee in 1964 that 'the image of the church as made up of bishops, priests and nuns is a grave misconception. The bishop is unfortunately regarded as "the church".' He added: 'We all are the church. We differ in function. Unfortunately in this country – for historical reasons – the bishop is regarded as the church. This concept will take years to eliminate.'[4]

A holy man
Interviewees stress Archbishop McQuaid's holiness. This is a difficult concept to describe, but for Vincent Gallagher, 'he oozed sanctity, you'd feel it in his presence'; Fr Butler: 'I felt that I was always in the presence of a holy man, I regarded this man as a man of prayer'; Canon Paddy Battelle: 'I would say he has a very high place in heaven because he always acted according to his conscience. Always a great man of principle.' Within six months of his death, groups of people were gathering each Sunday around his tomb in Dublin's Pro-Cathedral, asking for his intercession and seeking his beatification.[5]

Three elements were used to define the nature of his holiness – faith, obedience and charity. Many have witnessed to the centrality of faith in his life. Ann Lee says he had 'great faith in his angel guardian'.

McQuaid, with Mgr MacMahon and Osmond Dowling, Diocesan Press Officer, drafted replies to questions from author Tim Pat Coogan in 1965. As to what books he read, they listed the classics, Latin and French, works of theology and scripture, especially of the French scholars; periodicals of theology, scripture and current affairs; also medicine and psychology. His favourite spiritual authors were St Thomas Aquinas, St John of the Cross, St Teresa of Avila and St Francis de Sales.[6] Some would be surprised that de Sales was a favourite, because de Sales' gentle approach, as writer and bishop of Geneva, and his preference to lead with honey rather than a stick, would seem in contrast to the perception of McQuaid as a strict, often harsh, disciplinarian. Tim Pat Coogan sent similar written questions to all of the Irish bishops, in research for a new book, but he did not receive the reply from McQuaid.[7] Fr Lehane, a past pupil of Blackrock College, remembering John Charles' regular visits to Rockwell, says 'He had a taste for good detective stories and Josephine Tey was an author he often recommended.'

He frequently recommended Francis de Sales to students at Holy Cross College, Clonliffe, the diocesan seminary, and one retired priest recalls how he gave him his own copy of de Sales' *Introduction to the Devout Life*. In 1955, at his suggestion, Dublin Institute of Catholic Sociology (DICS) introduced a course in ascetical theology with *Introduction to the Devout Life* as the core textbook.[8]

Cardinal Connell believes that, for McQuaid, obedience was the ultimate test of holiness. He was obedient himself, with absolute certitude, to the instructions and wishes of the Pope, seeing this as the will of God, even when he didn't like it. Cardinal Connell tells how a priest once said to McQuaid that a certain other priest was a very holy man, and he asked: 'How do you know he is holy?' and further: 'Does he obey?' Mgr Conor Ward, retired Professor of Social Science, University College Dublin (UCD), believes that obedience to the church and its hierarchical system explained a lot of McQuaid's actions.

There are indications that his obedience and loyalty were appreciated by Pope Paul VI, as seen from his note in January 1966 to Amleto Cardinal Cicognani, Secretary of State:

> This afternoon I have received by air-freight from Milano a case of exquisite confectionary (*sic*) with a Christmas Card from His Holiness ... It is but another stimulus to a filial loyalty in which I trust I shall never, with God's help, be found wanting.[9]

The Archbishop's charity, especially his kindness to people in trouble, was praised in many interviews, Mgr Greene, for instance, saying: 'I always thought that he was a very humble man, a very charitable man. Charity was the keynote of his priesthood.'

Spiritual writers do not regard abstemiousness as essential for holiness, but it has often been a feature of holy people. Fr Tony Gaughan, parish priest, remembers McQuaid as 'so obviously abstemious and totally committed to his job. He lived for it.' He recalls his parish visits for confirmations and, at dinner afterwards, he would be 'at the top of table, fiddling with a bit of boiled chicken and then a bit of rice. And then a cup of tea.' Others also remember this. Canon Battelle says 'He might take a few sips of wine. Just a few sips. He was very abstemious. He seemed to eat very little ... He always had the chicken and the rice.' Fr Lehane says he never drank [alcohol] on his visits to

Rockwell but, as so often with McQuaid stories, there was the quirky side: 'He felt competent to judge the bouquet on a glass of wine ...'

Spiritual certitude

Archbishop McQuaid's then spiritual director, and Holy Ghost colleague, Fr Denis Fahey, wrote in 1930, admonishing him for continuing to seek certitude in his private, spiritual life, in his relationship with God. Achievement of this certitude always escaped him, as was inevitable, and it may have contributed to the insecurity, the uncertainty, with which he approached his final judgement with God.

Fr Fahey, a controversial, right-wing writer, whom McQuaid opposed in later years, in this case advised the young priest on the weakness in his approach to God and how he could improve in his spiritual life:

> Our Lord wants you *to turn your gaze and your energy upward* in faith in Him and he wants you not to seek to get sense-assurance ... You always aim at accuracy in speech and rightly ... Now, I have been trying to combat your tendency to get satisfaction for sense faculties' demand for assurance and you have, very often, in the phase after you had promised to look upward to Our Lord and keep your gaze on Him and on His Interests *first*, slipped back again ... I say this because you are inclined to seek for intellectual certitude as to *your* exact position in the spiritual life. That is secondary altogether to the question whether Our Lord finds you ever looking at this side of all events, irrespective of self.[10]

McQuaid remained a man of prayer and this is reflected in his pastoral letters. It is possible he never managed to follow Fr Fahey's advice, but kept slipping back and worrying about not being able to achieve personal spiritual certitude. Some did not like the firm hand with which he ruled his diocese but he was consistent and predictable, with intellectual certitude that he was always right and it was his duty to rule in this way. John Cooney refers to his 'unshakeable certitude that his path in life, though not without its share of emotional tumult and unexpected directions, was guided by Jesus Christ.'[11]

Telling him the truth

His strong certitude about everything and his rigorous attitudes may have led some priests, and others, to tell him not the full truth but only what they thought he wanted to know. There is evidence, however, that he wanted to be told the truth. He told his Public Image Committee they were not to hold back any-thing in their report. As Mgr MacMahon reported from the com-mittee:

> There was no use asking people for an opinion unless they could feel free to give it. They were not to think that anything they felt ought to be said would hurt. It would not. His Grace reminded the meeting of their duty to point out anything that is defective because if they did not they must render an account for it at their judgement.[12]

Fr Roland Burke Savage, a Jesuit friend and editor of *Studies*, on being blamed for the embarrassment over the Mansion House ecumenical meeting in 1966 (see Chapter 6), wrote to McQuaid:

> ... unlike many of your own clergy and laity, I was never two-faced, saying what you wanted to hear in your presence and cutting you to ribbons behind your back. Nor could it ever be said that I tried to serve you for any base motive, as Your Grace's friendship could not do anything for me as it could for your own clergy.[13]

The reply was a sharp one:

> For my clergy and laity 'who tell me what they think I want to know and cut me to ribbons behind my back', I do not know these persons, fortunately. Treachery is inherent in the clergy since the days of Our Divine Redeemer. But I can say this: The amount that I receive from clergy or *laity* that could be called even consoling is very small; the amount that is laudatory extremely small. I can indeed deceive myself, but not all the time, more especially as I am acutely aware that judgement cannot be distant.[14]

When Otto Herschen of *The Catholic Herald* told McQuaid he disagreed with the decision to remove modernistic figures from the Christmas crib at Dublin Airport church, McQuaid replied: 'I am glad you disagree. Everyone else agrees with whatever I say.'[15]

Insecurity

McQuaid's certitude in faith, in obedience and in all of his statements and actions would seem unquestionable, but Fr Gaughan believes his shyness and sometimes overbearing manner were a cover for what was an insecurity and that he had doubts himself and about himself which he never revealed. He often spoke of the importance of one's mother, an example being given by Mgr Greene: 'I said, "Your episcopal ring is a very nice thing", and he said, "That's my mother's ring, I had a stone inserted into it. They always said to me, 'always cherish your mother'. You only have one mother. Always keep her very much in mind".' His mother, Jenny, died, aged 22, just days after his birth and he did not know until he was 16 that his stepmother, Agnes, was not his natural mother. Cooney speculates, without evidence, that this could have been a source of his insecurity.[16]

The extensive correspondence from Archbishop Finbar Ryan in Trinidad to Archbishop McQuaid shows that both men had the same outlook on religious matters, as when Ryan wrote in 1959:

> … the Catholic educational machinery which you have set in motion in Dublin is the greatest contribution to the fulfilment of our Patrician destiny that could be made. I wish I could be sure that this is appreciated in Ireland and in Rome. Don't weaken.[17]

The RTÉ television documentaries on the opening of the McQuaid archives feature a voice-over at the beginning which was not identified to viewers.[18] It was Mgr Tom Fehily. The interviews had been completed and the cameras turned off, but the sound was still on and Mgr Fehily spoke, unrehearsed and unprompted, not aware he was being recorded. The director kept the sound going. This story was repeated by Mgr Fehily for this research, with slight amendments and a final sentence:

> I saw him shortly before he died and he said: 'I am very frightened of dying.' And I said: 'Your Grace, why would you be frightened?' He said: 'Why wouldn't I be, Father?' …

'Well', I said, 'when you think of all the things you did' and I listed all the extraordinary work he did for the poor and the new parishes he established and the new churches he built, all that sort of thing, the number of religious orders he brought in, the number of new colleges he founded, etc. He said, 'Father, all of that may be true but not one of those are mentioned at your judgement, not one of them.' He said: 'You are only asked ... with what love did you do what you did? Love of me or love of your own promotion? I don't know the answer and that's why I am worried.' And then I said to him: 'Ah, Your Grace, I am sure that everything will be grand at your judgement', and he said: 'Father, dear, and who' – I remember it so clearly – 'Father, dear, and who gave you permission to sit in the judgement seat of God?'

McQuaid made frequent references to the final judgement. When Louis McRedmond, in 1970, sought an interview with him for *The Irish Times*, he declined but commented: 'You are kind to write in such a strain, but I must wait for the judgement of God on that chapter, a merciful judgement, I hope, for myself and for all with whom I have had to deal or who have dealt with me.'[19] When Fr Burke Savage was planning to write his biography, he hoped he would

be far beyond its reach and the reaction that it will arouse on earth. And, by then, I shall have learned, in judgement, the genuine *chiaroscuro* of my poor image before God. *Unicus et pauper* I shall certainly be in that moment, so keep on praying for me in your gentle charity.[20]

He wrote to Fr Burke Savage in 1966: '... I can indeed deceive myself, but not all the time, more especially as I am acutely aware that judgement cannot be distant.'[21] When he addressed his all-priest Public Image Committee in January 1964, he reminded them of their duty to point out anything that was defective in the diocese because if they did not 'they must render an account for it at their judgement'.[22]

Finally, as he was dying in Loughlinstown Hospital, Dublin, he rose from the pillow and, as told to John Cooney, asked staff nurse Margaret O'Dowd 'if he had any chance of reaching heaven.

She told him that if he, as Archbishop could not get to heaven, few would. This answer appeared to satisfy him and he lay back on the pillow to await death.'[23]

Wide knowledge and precision

Many confirm McQuaid's wide general knowledge, an 'encyclopedic knowledge' on a lot of issues that weren't associated with the church. Bishop Donal Murray of Limerick, who was a Dublin priest in the 1960s, says it was 'probably from many years teaching … that might have been part of it … he had a huge capacious kind of mind … an absolutely photographic memory'. Canon Battelle mentions his precision and thoroughness in everything and how he expected the same from others: 'He was meticulous in checking out information … He was the most magnificent time-keeper you ever came across.'

He could be a genial and interesting host. In January 1962, he had Ed Roth, Director General of Telefís Éireann, Michael Barry, Director of Programmes and Eamonn Andrews, Chairman, for dinner at his home in Killiney and they all wrote appreciative letters of thanks. Roth said how he 'particularly enjoyed the informal and extremely interesting conversation with you after dinner … and may I say Your Grace's selection of cigars is excellent'.[24]

McQuaid always dressed in formal episcopal attire and insisted that all clerics, not just his own priests and students, must at all times wear their hats out of doors. Vincent Gallagher remembers how at Blackrock College '… he was always impeccable. You would never see the man in casual wear …'. He was strong on traditional etiquette, always, for instance, writing his letters by hand and expecting the same in return. The archives show Osmond Dowling's letters to him from the Diocesan Press Office were always handwritten, as were those from his fellow bishops. His own spidery, upright handwriting was small, but legible, and it never wavered. Mgr Ward's understanding was that 'I should always handwrite my letters to him and that he would handwrite them back.'

Gentle and courteous, cold and austere

In some ways he was a complex man and John Feeney, the radical UCD student and journalist, was probably accurate when he referred to the man and the mask.[25] Those closest to him tend to say he was gentle and courteous, while many at a distance share a perception that he was cold and austere. For Ann Lee: '... a very gentle person ... a very courteous man, to everybody'; for Fr Butler: '... ever so gentle ... And his manners, they were impeccable'. Fr Lehane emphasises courtesy, as in the brief letters of thanks he received after every visit the archbishop made to Rockwell. Fr Lehane also remembers him, on one occasion, just arrived at Rockwell, sitting on the side of his bed, dangling his feet, looking at the coal fire, and saying 'This is heaven.' Margaret McMahon, a close friend, described him as 'extremely likeable ... when you went into the room it was like as if there was an infrared heater on'.[26] He told John H. Whyte, in one of his rare interviews, that a Belgian friend, often under attack, once told him: 'It is never permitted to one to be discourteous.'[27]

Fr Chris Mangan, secretary to the archbishop from 1941 to 1957, found him to be an 'exceptional' man, the 'kindest man I ever met or lived or worked with...' He saw him as a 'warm and even emotional man, kind and compassionate with a wide range of interests and friendships'. He told McQuaid, on appointment, that he wasn't going to say he agreed with what he said if he didn't agree. Nor was he going to say things just to please him. 'He agreed with me ... he would bristle sometimes when I acted that way, even then I would find him doing the things that I said.'[28]

McQuaid was meticulous in replying immediately to correspondence. It must therefore have grieved him when the Papal Nuncio, Mgr Giuseppe Sensi, once wrote about two letters from the previous month to which he had not replied. His immediate note on Sensi's letter read: 'Ansd. I regret very much that Your Excellency should have been obliged to write me. The simple truth is that I have, at this season, been very hard pressed at work.'[29] As he told Fr Lehane that he never let anybody else open his letters, this is surprising. Was it a sign he was weakening, or had been ill, or did his loyalty to others cause him to cover up an oversight?

Mgr Jerome Curtin asserts that the image of McQuaid in Blackrock College was not the aloofness and remoteness often associated with him as archbishop: 'He was the most popular member on the staff', although never in terms of being 'hail-fellow-well-met'. Vincent Gallagher says 'he knew every pupil, every boarder in the school' and there seemed to be a magnetism about him. Gallagher recalls another boy saying to him one evening: 'Aren't we lucky to be here, during the time, the term of the Mickser – we called him Mickser – because he is a man in a million.' Fr Dermod McCarthy, Religious Programmes Editor, Radio Telefís Éireann, as a student in Clonliffe College, was another who noticed this appeal: 'There was a bit of a Mona Lisa look about him. You weren't sure whether he was smiling or not. But he had a magnetic presence.'

Fr Gaughan believes he never shook off the schoolmasterly, stand-offish manner, that one can develop as part of imposing discipline on others: 'And I suppose, unconsciously, if you are like that for a number of years, your formative years, you tend to continue that way.'

His closest friends were aware of the aspects in his manner which were criticised by others. One of them admits that people would say he tended to be a bit sharp and caustic in his style, especially in written communications. Canon Battelle refers to the stiff upper lip, 'because he wanted to be so correct and he never wanted to show anybody that basically he had any feelings at all'.

For broadcaster Gay Byrne, the 'ogre' aspect to which McQuaid himself referred at the opening of the Diocesan Press Office, was enhanced by his style at ceremonies in the Pro-Cathedral and at confirmations: 'The crowds would be out in force and genuflecting and an altar boy holding the ends of the long *cappa magna*. And again, the austere pose.' A senior parish priest remembers '… a terrible awe and … he swept into a sacristy … people were afraid of him … that was the kind of atmosphere he created. Publicly, anyhow…'. John Horgan, former Professor of Journalism, Dublin City University, but then on the staff of *The Irish Times*, has the impression that 'he cultivated this image that he projected to the world of the austere, remote, unapproachable figure. I think probably because it enhanced his authority, or he felt that it enhanced his authority.' Horgan never had a private conversation with him, but believes that underneath this austerity he could be 'quite impish, almost, and taking a delight in how people were affected by the outward mien that he adopted'.

The Public Image Committee (1964) described a strong public image of the archbishop, in the light of which everything he said or did was coloured, even if it was not a 'true image':

> The public image of the Archbishop of Dublin is entirely negative: a man who forbids, a man who is stern and aloof from the lives of the people, a man who doesn't meet the people (as they want him to) at church functions, at public gatherings, or television or in the streets, who writes deep pastoral letters in theological and canonical language that is remote from the lives of the people.[30]

Shy, remote, formal
John Charles' shyness is a consistent theme in the interviews. Derek Scott thinks he was 'basically a shy man. It wasn't easy to have a conversation with him. He would say something to you and you would say something back and he might just suddenly move on to the next person.' Fr Butler believes that '… people's distance from him, which he was aware of, didn't help him at all with regard to overcoming his shyness'. For Fr Gaughan, he was 'pathologically shy, he was a very, very shy person … But apart from that, he had a difficulty in communicating with fellow-adults.'

Cardinal Connell believes he 'found it hard at events like confirmation', and Fr Eltin Griffin, a Carmelite priest who ministered in Whitefriars Street Dublin city parish in the 1960s, agrees: 'He didn't go in for photographs after confirmation or anything like that.' However, when correcting the proofs for Fr Burke Savage's article in *Studies*, he wrote: 'I think it inaccurate that I dislike ceremonies.'[31]

The Public Image Committee reported in 1964 that 'our bishops are very remote' and they pointed at their own archbishop, suggesting that

> the formation of a positive image may be assisted by the cumulative effect of little things such as sedulous meeting of parents after confirmation, appearing informally on televi-

sion, allowing informal press photographs and in general, in so far as is possible, by dropping the formal manner.[32]

It would be easy to attribute this formality to shyness, but, for Cardinal Connell, 'that was not peculiar to Archbishop McQuaid. That was the custom of the time, that kind of formality.' Mgr Patrick Corish, retired President and Professor of Ecclesiastical History, St Patrick's College, Maynooth, says that 'in those days everyone was formal. All men wore hats, or if they were lower class they wore caps. He came from that sort of world ...'.

Loyalty, obedience and control
Older priests, in particular, had an intense loyalty to John Charles and they remembered the reforming zeal with which, from his first days in office, he reorganised the entire adminis-tration of the diocese and the many charitable and other activi-ties in which it was engaged, with special attention to the poor and the needy. Priests still emphasise the mutual loyalty which overrode other aspects of their relationship with him. They speak of how he recognised social issues such as drug-taking be-fore many of the politicians and acted on them. Fr Butler says the priests were 'a loyal group' and despite the fact that many of them might not 'love' their archbishop, they 'respected' him. Fr Gaughan says 'He was tremendously loyal to his priests, and that meant they were loyal to him.' Bishop Murray also testifies to this loyalty but is not sure to what extent it was a 'personal loyalty ...'. Canon Battelle says they criticised him and were often unhappy with him, but 'all had a loyalty to him ...'. Fr Dermod McCarthy says his late uncle, Sean Carey, a parish priest, felt to the end that John Charles was 'perfectly right in everything he did. He had a huge loyalty.' Vincent Gallagher re-members another priest in the 1960s, whose 'admiration for McQuaid was absolute, he could see no wrong in the archbishop. He also had a Cavan background.' Mgr Ward, when asked if McQuaid had a high degree of loyalty from his priests, replies that 'he got a high degree of obedience' and this was a sort of 'ours-not-to-reason-why' style of obedience.

McQuaid had definite views on how authority should be exercised in the church. Reporting the first meeting of the Public Image Committee, Mgr Ardle MacMahon noted that 'the archbishop announced as a matter of principle that authority cannot give its reasoning'. When Fr Burke Savage replied that the tendency today is for people to be interested in the reason for events, the archbishop replied: 'People must accept decisions because authority has spoken, and not for the reasons behind the decision. This is, of course, because authority is from God, and the voice of authority is the voice of God.' The Committee disagreed with him in their final report: 'Knowledge about the background to public actions and the reasons for the decisions is regarded as a vital step in the creation and maintenance of a public image. Currently people appear to "need" reasons and background information ... Also, an enlightened obedience appears to be more successful than an unreasoned assent.'[33]

A word frequently used in these interviews to describe Archbishop McQuaid's management of the diocese, of people, and of himself, is 'control', even 'control-freak'. Clerical and lay interviewees, friends and 'enemies', those close to him and even those who only knew him from a distance, stress this. Cardinal Connell saw him as 'very much the man in control' and a senior parish priest says 'every single thing was controlled by him'. Mgr Owen Sweeney remembers that his messages to the priests at their annual retreat tended to emphasise discipline, with sets of warnings, admonitions and prohibitions and 'deprecate' as a recurring word. This would be the same message as many of the laity took from some of his pastoral letters and his annual Lenten Regulations.

Some have criticised him for transferring priests suddenly to remote and less desired parishes, as a punishment or sign of his displeasure, with never an explanation, just the formal typed letter. Others say that was the norm for everybody. Nobody was given a reason for their move. Mgr Fehily was moved suddenly and without explanation from his position as Director of the Dublin Institute of Catholic Sociology. It was seen as a sacking, but no reason was ever given. It seems that he was blamed over some event that went wrong while McQuaid was in Rome for the Vatican Council. Somebody seems to have reported him and McQuaid acted at once despite their close and trusted relationship. He gave him a hint that he would be getting a letter in the post and that he would not like it and told him that this was the first time he had given a priest such a hint: 'I am making an exception as a token of my gratitude.' It appears that the report was a false one but Mgr Fehily will never tell anyone whom he believes was responsible, adding that the move back to full-time parish work was the best thing that ever happened to him. Six months later, he was invited, through his parish priest, to the archbishop's south Dublin residence in Killiney. John Charles met him at the door and said:

> 'Father, before we have lunch may I, will it be all right, if we have a little walk.' And I said: 'Certainly, Your Grace', and he said, 'If I was to say to you, Father, that I have suffered more in the last six months than you have, can we leave it at that?', and 'it' was never mentioned again.

David Sheehy refers to this weakness in McQuaid, how 'like a capricious dictator, he could also summarily dismiss favoured priests from their posts on the basis of a misunderstanding or in response to false information fed by courtiers, the accuracy of which he failed independently to verify.'[34]

Fear and awe

Mgr Stack says many older, as well as younger priests, were 'terrified' of the archbishop: 'There was this air about him. It might have been a filial fear … I know priests who were summoned to his presence for not wearing a hat, and they were terrified.' This fear often came from their student days. Mgr Stack does not believe there was a 'regime of terror', their faith and understanding of the church and what they were at meant they did not construe it in that way: 'We weren't going around neurotically worried all the time about the archbishop … life went on …'. Fr Butler found 'people were inclined to be a bit scared of him'. Mgr Greene knew him well, and was not fearful of him, 'but I would watch my Ps and Qs'.

Journalist John Brophy's parish priest in Donnybrook was Fr Cyril P (Paddy) Crean, a Second World War chaplain who had been on the beaches in Normandy, 'and people like that could still be made quake in their boots when the archbishop came …'.

Publisher Michael Gill remembers Edward Canon Gallen, the ecclesiastical censor, was 'absolutely terrified of the archbishop'. Joseph Foyle plays down the element of fear: 'They were part of the same mould ... they knew what his style was and how to keep on the right side of him.' The Public Image Committee considered that, while priests respected McQuaid, 'they are afraid of him, even some parish priests'.[35]

Fr Joe Dunn, through the Radharc film unit, had regular dealings with John Charles and

> I became fond of him. I got on well with him, relatively speaking and judging by some of the stories that other priests tell. I'm also grateful to him because I owe him a lot. That said, I must also say that there was no man that I feared more. He exercised absolute power over his priests which nobody in their right mind would dare question.[36]

Fr Dermod McCarthy remembers 'a sense of great awe going into the presence of this man' and when he swept through the Pro-Cathedral or the corridors of Clonliffe, 'with his black cloak just touching the ground ... it was a rather awesome sight'. Fr McCarthy remembers how, even in a friendly meeting, this sense of awe put one on the defensive: 'He had gimlet eyes and I can see him sitting behind the desk, gently touching his finger-tips together and phrasing questions in an unusual way ...'. He gives an example from his own student days in Clonliffe when the archbishop, after the summer holiday, 'instead of saying, "Had you a good summer?" or "What did you do over the summer holidays?" would ask, "How were you during the summer?" – and he didn't mean my physical health. It forced one to pause and think!'

Bishop Murray speaks of 'a bit of awe' in his relationship with him and that one would be 'uneasy' with him. He believes many priests shared that awe. Mgr Greene says Mgr Joseph Carroll, President of Clonliffe College and Auxiliary Bishop of Dublin, always referred to the archbishop as the 'High Command' and would say, 'never offend the High Command'. Awe could become 'obsequiousness' and Fr Gaughan says some priests went so far that it became embarrassing. He sees it as a 'black mark' against McQuaid and a 'touch of vanity' that he allowed it. Fr Dermod McCarthy found it 'quite revolting' in some of the older priests.

Kindness

It is a feature of the enigma of John Charles McQuaid that he could be severe while at the same time having a deserved reput-ation for kindness to priests and laity, legendary for his visits to the hospitals and assisting everybody whom he found in need. This good work was usually done quietly and without publicity and it has been asserted that his naïvete at times led to him being duped by tricksters who made up hard luck stories.

Interviewees mentioned his kindness as much as they men-tioned anything else. Canon Battelle says he 'always did every-thing possible to help ... in a very quiet, private way'; a retired priest says how 'where someone went to him in trouble, they really got an open door'; Cardinal Connell remembers how con-siderate and helpful he was to priests who sought laicisation and that included financial help so they could make a fresh start. Mgr Greene says: 'If he heard of any sick priest, or any sick friend, or a friend of a priest, or a friend of a friend, he would al-ways go to see them.'

In 1969, when John H. Whyte was completing his landmark book, *Church & State in Modern Ireland, 1923-1970,* Archbishop McQuaid gave him an extensive interview of more than three hours, with dinner, at his residence in Killiney. Whyte found him completely at ease, and not at all on the defensive: 'I had dif-ficulty afterwards in reconciling this courteous and kindly gen-tleman with the waspish letters and verbal rebukes which I know him to have produced.' He did, however, find McQuaid 'rather pre-occupied with his "enemies".'[37]

His 'enemies'

He frequently referred to his attackers as his 'enemies', both in conversation and in correspondence. Fr Burke Savage tried to answer the criticisms that he was 'too aloof from his flock, anti-Protestant, anti-liturgical, anti-artistic, interferes in the affairs of UCD and a meddler in politics'.[38] He then suggested that, 'de-spite the clamour of vocal critics, the number of his enemies is few indeed'.[39] Fr Burke Savage meant well but, by raising these points so succinctly, he seems to have provided ammunition for the 'enemies'.

When McQuaid referred to 'my enemies', they were not just his enemies in Dublin, but in Rome also. Bishop Patrick Dunne, his Auxiliary, wrote to him from Italy, September 1958, referring to Archbishop Alfonso Carinci's secretary with a 'bundle of literature for Your Grace. She is a Signora Castiglione-Masero, a widow, I should think.' McQuaid noted: 'What a strange interview, with a strange secretary: If I had a widow for Secretary what would not my enemies say at Rome. And they have, as I know, put in a lot of work on me already.'[40]

He was a subject of attack, especially in *The Irish Times*, from long before the 1960s and the Second Vatican Council. Much of it was rooted in the part he played in the Mother and Child issue in 1950 and his meetings and correspondence with the Minister for Health, Dr Noël Browne, which led to Browne's resignation and the government withdrawing the scheme which would have given free healthcare to all children up to 16 years of age. Despite this, he told John H. Whyte that over 29 years he found a complete absence of contention between church and state, they were 'very pleasant years' and he received courtesy and co-operation.[41]

In 1965, an attack by *Irish Times* columnist Myles na gCopaleen (Brian O'Nolan) nearly led to a libel case, but McQuaid, and his legal advisers, declined to proceed.[42] There had been references by Myles in his *Irish Times* column to Merrion Square (purchased for the diocese by Edward Byrne, the previous archbishop) and an old debate over whether it might be the site for a new Catholic Cathedral. Osmond Dowling had written a long reply which seems to have added fuel to the fire, as Myles then came back in his 'George Knowall' column in the Carlow paper, *The Nationalist & Leinster Times*:

> ... In Dublin there are tens of thousands of poorish people living and trying to rear families in slums, not infrequently competing for accommodation with rats, while all over the area (though admittedly in the tonier parts) abound solid, princely often towering buildings housing communities of nuns doing absolutely nothing all day (apart from getting

outside at least three square meals) but giving glory to God … Every parish teems with male clergy who, apart from morning ecclesiastical duties, mostly on Sundays, have practically nothing to do with their time, thanks to State social services and highly organised lay charities.[43]

McQuaid told Fr Burke Savage, from Rome: 'You should watch the Carlow paper. I have seldom seen anything worse than George Knowall's letter on the priests and nuns of Dublin. (He is, I am assured, Myles na gCopaleen).'[44] He instructed Dowling not to get into correspondence with the *Nationalist*, and referred to the 'unfortunate letter of O. G. Dowling that provoked' this attack. There was some concern and McQuaid's solicitor, Edward G. Gleeson, wrote:

… My thoughts on reflection and reasoning could fill some pages but may I just say that I am of the view that at the moment there is no positive step – overt or otherwise which can usefully or wisely be taken.

If and when another 'attack' comes the problem must be reviewed in the light thereof and my opinion then may be different. I say this because sooner or later a stand may have to be made against this insidious type of thing.

McQuaid noted: 'Very grateful. I have never defended myself, nor should I, unless the office of archbishop were attacked. Mgr [Cecil] Barrett will be a good consultant.'[45] Mgr Barrett said McQuaid's 'silence on the occasion of criticism has been commented on with wonder and even regret.'[46]

Myles na gCopaleen did not long survive the controversy. Just a few months later, Dowling told the archbishop: 'I did not attend poor Myles' funeral, as I did not know him personally and thought my presence might be misconstrued, so I just said a prayer instead.'[47] O'Nolan, who also had the *nom-de-plume* of Flann O'Brien, was a pupil at Blackrock when McQuaid was Dean of Studies. John Cooney says he imitated McQuaid's writing and provided his versions to other boys as official excuses for undone home work.[48]

Attacks increased through the 1960s with, notably, *The Manchester Guardian*, and *Herder Correspondence* publishing articles which criticised the way Archbishop McQuaid ruled his diocese and his alleged slowness in bringing in changes after the Second Vatican Council.

He commented to Fr Burke Savage about Peter Lennon's articles in *The Manchester Guardian*, which referred to him as a 'Grey Eminence': 'I find it hard to understand the venom. It is very untrue, from my own knowledge of my own actions … I think that the Faith will not suffer, and that alone counts.'[49] He told John Watt, a former UCD lecturer, who defended him in a letter to *The Manchester Guardian* that the Lennon article 'is so severe that I am encouraged to hope that it will not really damage the Faith, and that is what alone counts.'[50] He also referred to Lennon when he addressed the Public Image Committee in the same month: 'Unfortunately this meeting coincides with a campaign concerning my method of dealing with affairs in the diocese. This is an epiphenomenon.'[51] Referring again to Lennon (who was from Dublin), he told Fr Burke Savage:

> This form of attack is another type of loneliness. But I hope with God's help and Our Lady's kindly assistance, to see in it only what God permits for his own purposes – very hidden purposes indeed. Ultimately my silence will be understood, but by then I shall be, I hope, with God.[52]

He confided again to Fr Burke Savage soon after: 'You do not think that I worry at these attacks and you are right. But the isolation they effect brings me, I hope, closer to Our Divine Lord.'[53] He regretted the Lennon attack, telling John Whyte: '…that poor lad whose mother and brother are daily communicants. His mother didn't go to her accustomed church for several weeks after those articles appeared.'[54]

In reply to his letter about media coverage and press criticism, Fr Burke Savage said he felt 'very sad' that he was suffering so much. Dr McQuaid underlined 'suffering so much' and noted 'This is an error' – in other words, he had not admitted to suffering.[55]

Herder Correspondence, July 1965, referred to a 'curial mentality' in the Dublin archdiocese and Archbishop McQuaid responding 'hesitantly to the new winds from Rome'. It raised all the common attacks on him and, by seeming to refute them, had the opposite effect of re-inforcing them, such as his 'innate hatred of

Protestants'. The Editor, Herbert Auhofer, sent complimentary copies around the diocese and apparently to every primary school teacher and, with his copy to McQuaid, he wrote: '... We hope that our article has laid some ghosts and will help to ease the way for your pastoral work in Dublin for which I respectfully wish you every success.'[56] Osmond Dowling replied to Auhofer:

> It is, as your article implies, paradoxical that the only diocese so far to implement the Vatican Decree on Mass Communications by establishing a full-time press office in charge of a layman should be accused of failing to appreciate the *aggiornamento* and of possessing a curial mentality.

In a self-memo, in June 1965, McQuaid said Bishop William Philbin of Down & Connor had seen *The Irish Times* report on the *Herder Correspondence* article and had told him some bishops were wondering for how long they should continue to send news items to *The Irish Times*. '" *The Irish Times* had been treating me shamefully.' I thanked him and made no suggestion...'.[58]

McQuaid was not enthused by novelist Edna O'Brien, some of whose works had questioned traditional attitudes towards Irish female sexuality in a hitherto unusually explicit fashion. She wrote an article in the British *Daily Telegraph* which criticised his rule over the Dublin archdiocese and said his 'attitude filters into secular life, affecting newspaper articles, censorship, football games, health schemes and debates by the students of University College, Dublin.' She referred to the ban on Catholics attending Trinity College, Dublin, without his permission, and said how she went there to see the *Book of Kells*,

> ... a thing I had not dared to do when I was a student in Dublin. There was the inference of sin. It is still a sin, according to His Grace the Archbishop, to enroll at this Protestant University; but with true Irish ambiguousness, his nephew and niece have been students there.

He wrote on his own copy of the article: 'A renegade and – a dirty one' and marked the paragraph about his nephew and niece at Trinity: 'Absolutely untrue.'[59]

Mgr MacMahon says:

> I think he was aware also that there were various sources of

criticism [of him] and some of these would have been inimi-
cal to the influence of the Catholic Church in this country.
About education and medicine. Areas like that where, obviously, the church had enormous influence in the Republic
and there would be people who would have been ideologi-
cally very different and would resent that and would take the
opportunity of voicing it.

Mgr MacMahon picks out *The Irish Times* and says it was the
archbishop's policy 'never to reply to that kind of criticism … I
suppose too it was a measure of his enormous influence.' Fr
Lehane says: 'When McQuaid was hit he took the suffering in
silence, but it hurt deeply.' He recalls that, at Rockwell, McQuaid
always had breakfast at 8.30 and 'as he entered the president's
study – where his meals were served – he would glance at the
headlines of the papers without picking them up and frequently
and wryly comment: "Who's attacking me today?"'

Some see this silence in the face of his critics as another sign
of McQuaid's holiness. One priest says a friend of his, who was
close to the archbishop, believed he accepted the criticism and
the attacks 'very humbly' and 'offered it up', regarding it as
'something that he had to put up with for the Lord, because he
had that sort of spirituality …'.

A comment in his pastoral letter for the 50th anniversary of
Pope Paul VI's ordination, June 1970, could be applied to himself:

> Like the Son of God on earth, it has been his lot to be misrep-
> resented, opposed, reviled and even hated. But is it not the
> promise of Jesus Christ, Our Lord, that the servant shall not
> be greater than his Master, and that men shall hate His faith-
> ful Apostles and disciples?[60]

He assured Fr Burke Savage that he would not be worried if
the *Studies* article, planned to commemorate his jubilee, led to
further attacks: '… If one has been a whipping post for years, another few strokes do not hurt so much. Besides, if God did not
permit all these comments, interpretations and calumnies, they
could not be uttered at all. Some good is meant by Him. And in
the end, He gets his way.'[61]

John Feeney, with his left wing group, Grille, was an unconventional critic of the archbishop, writing to the newspapers to apologise to other Christians for the unecumenical tones of one of his pastoral letters on church unity, picketing Clonliffe College because of plans to rebuild it at a time of serious housing shortage in the city, and attacking him, on the RTÉ television *Late Late Show* for introducing planned giving for parish collections.[62] Gay Byrne, the host of the show, then described McQuaid as 'the most maligned man in the country'.[63] Feeney attacked McQuaid as a man 'hated' by considerable sections of his priests and laity and 'an isolated remnant of an earlier more strident era in Irish Catholicism'.[64] Feeney was milder, though still very critical, when he 'regretted the ease by which the faults of so many Catholics were all laid at the door of one single man who had reached an age when few people find it easy to break from the old ways'[65] and he summed up McQuaid as 'a great churchman, a great leader, and more important than all, a great follower of Christ'.[66]

Until the establishment of the Diocesan Press Office in 1965 the archbishop sent his press information to the *Irish Independent* and *Irish Press* but not always to the *The Irish Times*. A note to from one of his secretaries, March 1962, says that year's pastoral was being given late to *The Irish Times* 'because last year the *Observer* (England) commented on the pastoral before it was issued and the *Observer* Correspondent is on *The Irish Times* staff.'[67]

While he 'offered up' personal criticism, he could respond sharply to anything that reflected on his priests and people. Two coincidental instances involved statements from Waterford diocese, one by Bishop Daniel Cohalan, who in 1943 preached a sermon about the neglect of the poor people in Dublin's Gardiner Street slums around the corner from the affluence of O'Connell Street, and again in 1966 when a Waterford priest alleged spiritual neglect of the people in the new suburb of Ballyfermot.[68]

The future John C. Cardinal Heenan of Westminster visited Dublin in 1941 and wrote critically in the *Catholic Herald* about the poor of Dublin being 'a living reproach to its citizens' and the poverty seeming to be regarded 'in too many circles with complacency'. He also found the young people to be 'sullen and resentful of the attitude of the clergy' and wondered whether the people's Catholic faith was 'a formality'.[69] John Cooney quotes Heenan and says how the criticism drew fire from McQuaid who wrote to Archbishop William Godfrey, Apostolic Delegate to Great Britain (also a future Cardinal of Westminster), saying the article had 'deeply angered both clergy and laity in the country'.[70]

A sense of humour
It surprises some that there is occasional reference in the interviews to John Charles' quaint sense of humour and numerous anecdotes, some of which are true and others endearingly apocryphal. There are references to his humour as 'sardonic' (Fr Gaughan); 'dry' (Mgr MacMahon); 'funny' (Bishop Murray) or 'quirky' (Gay Byrne) and to the 'twinkle in the eye' (Ann Lee, Fr Butler). There are moments of humour in his correspondence. Antrim were in the All-Ireland hurling final at Croke Park in September 1943 and their local Bishop, Daniel Mageean of Down & Connor, was invited to throw in the ball. He wrote to McQuaid, as was the usual courtesy in another bishop's diocese, for his permission. McQuaid's note: 'Certainly. Throw it in.'[71]

Derek Scott recalls a well-known incident with the sixth year boys in Blackrock College which was passed down to him. McQuaid had a limp and one boy, who was a good mimic, was performing in front of the class and strolling around with the limp and a good imitation of the voice when there was a tap on his shoulder: 'The limp is in the other leg.' Mgr Greene notes a 'great' sense of humour, recalling a confirmation dinner when McQuaid put on a cap and described the people who went to Croke Park [gaelic games], to Dalymount Park [soccer] and Lansdowne Road [rugby].

Bishop Murray believes John Charles got on well with the other bishops without saying much at the meetings, but what he said had impact and influence on decisions because he was bishop for one quarter of the population. He tells the story of him going into a meeting at Maynooth when a priest said to him: 'What does Archbishop Walsh [of Tuam] have in his bag? and McQuaid replied: "Spanners, Father".'

John Whyte saw a relaxed and, and at times, humorous McQuaid during their long interview over dinner in 1969. He was at ease and 'smiled often', laughing when he referred to the late Education Minister, Donogh O'Malley, as 'that tempestuous character' but adding he was a very good man to do business with.

CHAPTER TWO

Pope John's Dream –
The Council is Announced

Ireland, in general, was unprepared for the Second Vatican Council, with the bishops apparently unaware of what it might involve, but seeds were being sown, which would help priests and laity to understand the years ahead for the Catholic Church and its role in the modern world, the most prominent of which were in two religious and social journals, *The Furrow* and *Doctrine & Life*.

On 25 January 1959, Blessed John XXIII announced his plan to convoke the Twenty-First Ecumenical Council, the first since Vatican I in 1869-1870. Joe Power, religious correspondent for the *Irish Independent*, remembers Archbishop McQuaid saying the church needed a breath of fresh air and he believes McQuaid's initial reaction to the Council was one of welcome. David Rice, then a young Dominican priest in Rome, refers to 'this sense of spring in the air ... this marvellous sense of freedom happening' and 'a tremendous sense of euphoria'. Fr Tom Butler saw the announcement as 'completely out of the blue'. Vincent Gallagher says it was a 'great surprise' and he didn't realise its significance at the time, 'but John XXIII was definitely a man inspired'.

Osservatore Romano, the semi-official Vatican daily newspaper, made no mention of the Council on the evening the Pope announced it and next day 'sandwiched it between two other items of far less importance', a diocesan synod for the city of Rome and an update of the Code of Canon Law. *La Civilta Cattolica*, a Jesuit bi-monthly, also with semi-official Vatican status, did not mention the Council until 2 May. Robert B. Kaiser, *Time* correspondent in Rome, said some could not believe the news of the Council because of the common perception that Councils went out with the definition of papal infallibility and that 'John's idea did not exactly galvanise the ecclesiastical bureaucrats' in the curial offices of the Vatican.[1]

The word 'ecumenical' and its association with the growing movement for re-union of the Christian churches, created an immediate expectation that this would be the purpose of the Council. These expectations were raised by elements in the Pope's announcement and by theologians, most prominently Fr Hans Küng.[2] For Fr Kevin McNamara, later Archbishop of Dublin, it was clear from the beginning that John XXIII saw 'in this hoped-for renewal of the church a great step forward on the road to Christian unity'.[3] Fr Michael Hurley, a prominent Jesuit ecumenist, suggested it would give 'a new fillip to Catholic ecumenism' and help 'certain present trends to establish themselves more deeply and above all to spread more widely'.[4]

Expectations

Charles McCarthy, an Irish trade union leader, identified the church going into the 1960s with 'immutable authority and inscrutable remoteness', where 'rules were our guide, at all times, our first introduction to God and the church, our final way of meeting him'. There was much talk of sin, heaven and hell, purgatory and limbo 'so that vast spiritual worlds were in travail over the close interpretation of a canonical provision'. It was a world 'full of legal traps' from which only God's mercy could rescue one. He added that Pope John then 'turned everything topsy turvy with an insight that has proved to be so devastatingly correct'.[5]

Louise Fuller has examined the pre-conciliar era in Ireland when bishops 'were very preoccupied with warning people about dangers to faith and morality', especially sexual morality, and feared threats to Irish Catholic culture coming from mainland Europe, an approach that was mainly reactive.[6]

The expectations of Archbishop McQuaid, and many of his priests, were based upon belief in the authority of the bishop and the duty of priests to give him absolute and uncritical obedience. New theological and social ideas were filtering into Ireland, but the expectation in 1959 was that there might be a gradual process of updating as had been seen during the long pontificate of Pope Pius XII (1939-58), but that nothing would change suddenly. Dublin diocesan priests were trained in Clonliffe College, divided by a wall from Archbishop's House,

Drumcondra. Some were sent for part of their studies to St Patrick's College, Maynooth, or to overseas universities, usually in Rome or Louvain. Philosophy students attended University College, Dublin (UCD) for a three-year BA degree.

Mgr Tom Stack remembers Clonliffe in the 1950s as 'cold, formal, kind of alienating ...'. He does not believe Archbishop McQuaid understood consultation, but priests didn't expect it because they had been formed in a 'non-consultative culture'. A retired priest still remembers the regime at Clonliffe as 'archaic' and 'very strict' without any attempt 'to put you in touch with modern conditions' and he criticises the theological teaching as 'old scholastic style' and very much confined to textbooks. Mgr Stack says it was 'a much more formal time' with a great sense of 'immutability' and ministers in government acted the same way as Archbishop McQuaid, as did business firms, law firms, living in a 'slightly Victorian age' where there was 'enormous reverence for authority ... people were very conscious of the need to be obedient servants ...'.

Archbishop Diarmuid Martin of Dublin says Clonliffe was a 'very difficult seminary' in the early 1960s, and 'like a prison' with visits every second week. He found the rules very petty, especially in the beginning, and for the first three years 'we had no music, no newspapers, no television'.[7] This was the way seminaries, on instructions from Rome, were organised in those days, as seen in numerous accounts, such as Küng.[8]

Canon Paddy Battelle, ordained 1956, says he and several other younger priests did not expect much to happen: 'We expected new definitions. We expected a new way of liturgy, but we never expected to spin into a completely new ethos of the priesthood and of the church and of relationships between bishops and priests and people'. Fr Butler felt things would change slowly, but not through a Council: 'We didn't know what to expect ... Nor did the bishops ... It was absolutely new territory.'

Mgr Patrick Corish says some priests wondered what Vatican II could do, as all had already been defined by previous councils and by the Pope. He believes some bishops were 'hermetically sealed'. Fr Austin Flannery, then editor of the Dominican journal, *Doctrine & Life*, found a feeling among a lot of Irish bishops and priests that 'we have a winning team, why change it?' Mgr Stephen Greene saw nothing wrong with the faith in Ireland at that time, '… and the place was redolent of religion … and the right thing to do. Then, like all councils, its aftermaths produced quite a lot of problems that were not there in Ireland.'

Ireland in the 1950s was dominated by the twin issues of emigration and unemployment. John Charles McQuaid was, for most of his people, a remote, even invisible figure, but he had a strong, authoritarian presence, and was believed to know and influence everything that was happening. Professor Tom Garvin has referred to him as 'a kind of ecclesiastical dictator of the Dublin archdiocese' who 'dominated much of its civic as well as its religious life in a quite extraordinary way'.[9] Much has been written about the historical power of the Catholic bishops in Ireland and their role in the twin struggles for political and religious independence. John Cooney refers to the 'awesome power exercised by the Catholic Church in Ireland in the mid-twentieth century'[10] and the criticism that it seemed to be 'the effective government of the country'.[11]

Several interviewees in this research used the term 'clericalism', for the Irish church of the 1950s, meaning everything was still left to the clergy. The laity had little part to play in running the parish or church affairs and they were quite happy, their only duties being, as Bishop Ernest J. Primeau of Manchester, New Hampshire, USA said, disapprovingly, at Vatican II, to 'believe, pray, obey, pay'.[12] Michael de la Bedoyere typified the 'clericalist layman' as one who believes that only the priest can do real Christian work, and he wants to help him.[13]

Broadcaster and writer, Seán MacRéamoinn, says what distinguished

> all the bishops from the rest of us … was a kind of remoteness … they belonged to a slightly different world … And if there was any relationship between bishops and people … they were condescending somewhat … But it seems to be part of … what was expected … that along with the mitre … you were put on a slightly different level and people would kiss your hand.

Former *Irish Independent* editor, Louis McRedmond, remembers the respect laity had for clergy and the 'awe of bishops' that was built into them: 'It wasn't a fear thing, it wasn't an imposition … this was what the Irish Catholic Church was about.' He agrees it was a 'culture', the bishops 'came out of these people and this is what people expected of bishops, that they would conduct themselves like bishops …'

Joe Fitz-Patrick, a Trinity College student in the 1960s, and later a public relations consultant, says the parish clergy's seminary training 'basically perpetuated this old, awful thing of the parish priest being a kind of martinet, totally on a pedestal, and totally removed from reality and especially the reality of the ordinary-day life of the Catholic'. Fitz-Patrick finds it strange that priests who 'were ordained to preach and evangelise' spent so much time at tasks that the laity could do equally well or better, such as discussing insurance and security. Canon Battelle found the laity 'very conservative' and 'quite happy to let the priests handle the church'.

Mgr Conor Ward says one cannot know what the Irish people expected from the Council nor to what extent they were ready for it: 'This was in the days before surveys. So, we just don't know.' He accepts, however, that the Irish people's response to the changes as they came over the next few years, would suggest that they 'probably' were ready. Elizabeth Lovatt-Dolan, a lay activist, experienced 'a great bubbling, a kind of enthusiasm, that things are going to be different, lay people are going to be taken seriously, and they are going to be included in decision-making'. Joseph Foyle holds that 'even John XXIII himself didn't know what he was walking into' and that the bishops thought it would be a 'cakewalk'. Seán Mac Réamoinn agrees that certain bishops thought the Council would be over 'very quickly, perhaps in one session.'

Preparing Dublin for the Council
Leo McAuley, Irish Ambassador to the Holy See, reported, in March 1960, that in Rome it was different now from the original excitement aroused by the announcement of Vatican II: 'Perhaps people no longer expect a great deal from the Council, certainly not any long step towards reconciliation with the Orthodox Church.' McAuley believed 'the liberal atmosphere clothing the

original project has been dissipated' and that it could 'all be over in a single session'.[14] Bishop Donal Murray, then a student in Maynooth, remembers

> somebody saying to me that the big thing that seemed to require consideration, as far as the faculty in Maynooth was concerned, was the interpretation of servile work ... [Mgr P. F.] Frank Cremin, God rest him, he thought the biggest problem was servile work which was a whole half of a Commandment which was not clear.

Mgr Cremin told Archbishop McQuaid he was 'rounding off for the Commission of the Council a *Studium* on the law of abstaining from servile work', and he thanked him for 'a learned contribution' that he had sent with an outline of theological topics.[15]

Signs of new thinking in parts of the European church in the 1950s were not always as evident as they seemed in retrospect. Michael Gill refers to countries like Germany and Holland where, for example, liturgical renewal pre-dated the Council by maybe ten years. He wonders was the Council cause or effect:

> I think it was an effect of what was happening anyway ... an awful lot was going on philosophically, and the same thing was coming through theologically, and inevitably you had somebody of great sensitivity like John XXIII who said, 'Let's do something about this.'

Mgr Ardle MacMahon, studying in Rome during the 1950s, did not see much sign of movements of thought: 'Pope Pius XII had opened up things a bit, in the liturgy of Holy Week, for example ... but Pope Pius XII was a bit worried by some of these ideas that were developing.' Mgr MacMahon refers to Pius' encyclical, *Humani Generis* (1950), which was a reaction to the new thinking, 'but that is the usual reaction, I think, the reaction of caution, the reaction of what possible dangerous directions could this take'.

For Mgr MacMahon, the only indication as to what would come up at the Council was the questionnaire sent out by the Central Committee for the Preparation of the Council, 'indicating various subjects to be treated of and there was nothing in those that would have indicated any very great change.' All of the bishops in the world received this questionnaire and there were 30 responses from Ireland – 24 of the 26 residential bishops, the Papal Nuncio, Mgr Antonio Riberi, two auxiliary bishops and three retired missionary bishops. Some submissions were brief, with McQuaid's three pages being the longest apart from the Nuncio and Bishop Eugene O'Callaghan of Clogher. The texts of all submissions were published by the Vatican but classified at that stage as 'sub secreto'.[16]

Archbishop McQuaid's response considered the matters of greatest concern to be the union of the 'separated brethren' with the Catholic Church and what the church could do for world peace and to halt the progress of the nuclear arms race.[17] He wanted a stronger affirmation of the Catholic position on original sin and its effects and he proposed condemnation of 'modern errors' such as evolution, polygenism [multiple origins of mankind rather than the single parents, Adam and Eve], existentialism, socialism and communism, as well as 'errors' in philosophy arising from linguistic analysis, logical positivism and theories of symbols. He wished for an infallible definition of the Blessed Virgin Mary as Mediatress of All Graces, and wanted clarification on the power and authority of residential bishops in their dioceses. He was concerned about 'situation ethics' and 'moral rearmament', errors against Christian marriage, need for uniformity on interpretation of servile work which was forbidden on a Sunday, greater uniformity in church 'holydays of obligation' and modification of the laws of fast and abstinence. He was also looking for revisions in the Code of Canon Law (1917), including clarification of the bishop's role towards lay associations and members of religious orders who worked in the diocese. He stressed the importance of clergy visiting the homes in their parishes so that they could know their people and look after them. He wanted the Vatican to notify bishops of its actions and decisions before releasing them to the secular media.

The bishops' submissions were to assist the commissions set up in Rome to prepare documentation for discussion at the Council. Nuncio Riberi asked Archbishop McQuaid for suitable names of bishops and priests, 'eminent for a holy life as well as for their exceptional and orthodox knowledge of philosophy,

theology and canon law', who could be considered for membership of these commissions.[18]

Minutes of the Irish bishops' regular meetings at Maynooth
make little, if any, reference to the Council in the lead-up to its
opening. What seems the first reference was at their final meeting before the Council opened, when they issued a prayer for its
success, urging priests to recite their Divine Office and laity to
say the Rosary daily for this intention.[19] Editions of the annual
Irish Catholic Directory show the main thing the bishops said to
the people before and during the Council was to pray for its success, but they never asked them to submit views and ideas for
consideration.

Theological training of priests has been highlighted as a negative influence in preparation for the Council. Mgr Corish sees
the pre-Council years as the 'end of a long tradition which was
beginning to suffer from rheumatism and affliction of the joints'.
He typifies that tradition as teaching theology from textbooks,
leading to the belief that one could always be certain about
everything. There was discussion but 'it did not disturb the
overall atmosphere of certainty'. One parish priest remembers
how 'the professor came in and he more or less translated the
Latin textbook ... Most of the guys didn't know a word of Latin
anyhow ... Terrible stuff'. However, this had started to change.
The same parish priest, in Rome in the 1950s, became aware of
the new theological thinking, and of theologians like Frs Yves
Congar, Henri de Lubac, Karl Rahner and others, 'who were influencing us'. He returned to teach theology in Clonliffe College,
'and it was absolutely marvellous'.

Agents of change
Interviewees raised spontaneously, and with enthusiasm, good
influences that helped them to understand and implement the
Council. *The Furrow* and *Doctrine & Life* were highly praised. *The
Furrow*, from the national seminary at Maynooth, was edited by
Canon Jerry McGarry. *Doctrine & Life*, edited from 1957 by Fr
Austin Flannery, was published by the Dominican order in
Dublin. Mgr Tom Stack, ordained 1959, sees *The Furrow* as being
'the most significant single thing' that would have prepared him
for the Council. He sees Canon McGarry as 'an extraordinary

prophetic figure', personifying 'the symbol of enlightenment, combined with common sense ...'. He also refers to McGarry managing 'to publish things that on the face of it would seem to undermine the traditional hierarchical structure'. For Fr Eltin Griffin, McGarry was 'a complete original'. For Canon Battelle, *The Furrow*, in particular, 'began to sow new ideas and also some ideas we mightn't have been too happy with ...'. Patrick Masterson, then lecturer in Philosophy and later President of UCD, says *The Furrow* was coming through with a lot of views, and the new ideas 'began to find a more popular outlet'. Seán MacRéamoinn said the new priests emerging around and after the time of the Council were not just the products of Maynooth but of *The Furrow*. Elizabeth Lovatt-Dolan believes both journals were 'immensely influential, but for a relatively small group of readers.' MacRéamoinn says the Irish response to the Council came entirely through journals such as these.

Dublin diocesan priests, especially those in teaching posts, rarely wrote for *The Furrow* and *Doctrine & Life*. One reason may have been their awareness that the archbishop did not trust the orthodoxy of *The Furrow* and was cautious also about *Doctrine & Life*. They preferred to keep their heads down for fear of a re-buke. McQuaid used to complain that Canon McGarry edited *The Furrow* in Maynooth which was in the Dublin archdiocese, but submitted it for approval, as church law allowed, to the neighbouring and less disapproving Bishop of Kildare & Leighlin in whose diocese it was printed. This annoyance continued to the end with Bishop Michael Browne of Galway, a close ally of McQuaid in many matters, agreeing about 'the unrest in faith' that was 'pervading' Maynooth and saying that 'we should – as bishops – strike at the roots. *The Furrow* in my opinion is doing harm and it should be made clear to Dr Lennon [Bishop of Kildare & Leighlin] that he should not allow his diocese to be an escape vent for heretics'.[20] Fr Flannery says when he was appointed editor of *Doctrine & Life*, his Provincial Superior got a letter from John Charles saying this was OK but, 'I hope he will be very careful about articles dealing with liturgy or education', and 'so far we have been spared the Dialogue Mass'.

Fuller believes both clergy and people would have been 'considerably disturbed by, and less prepared for, the profound changes instigated by the conciliar reforms' were it not for *The Furrow* and *Doctrine & Life*.[21] Mgr Michael Olden, reviewing Fuller's book in *The Furrow*, says *The Furrow* 'did much to prepare the soil' for Vatican II and when the call to change came 'there was a degree of readiness to respond'.[22]

Flannery's 'Group'

An informal group, mainly of lay people, used come together with Fr Flannery for small discussion sessions. Some referred to them as 'Flannery's Harriers'. He says it arose from his friendship with Jack Dowling, a broadcaster and journalist:

> ... Jack was very keen to have theological discussions and I felt I couldn't cope with Jack without help. Gradually that grew into the idea of having a group, not a group with a priest in charge, but a group of lay people and priests ... We got people talking on subjects that John Charles wouldn't have liked ... There was very little theological discussion in Ireland, very little. And the result was when the bishops went to Rome they were ill-prepared ... and some of the things that were said came as a hell of a shock.

Joe Fitz-Patrick says meetings of The Group kept him 'sane and alive' so he could 'meet with Catholic intellectuals, discuss current affairs, that maybe things might change'. Patrick Masterson went occasionally and it would be 'a ferment for theological discussion'. It was reported to Fr Flannery that the archbishop said: 'I believe Fr Flannery has a *salon* in my diocese.' There was no further reaction. He never wrote to them nor said anything at all.

Milltown Park public lectures

Series of public lectures were held at the Jesuit College, Milltown Park, Dublin every spring and winter from 1960 to 1969 inclusive. Fr Michael Hurley, the organiser, says they were 'highly significant' in educating the laity: 'Their success in attracting audiences clearly indicated they met a need.' Fr Eltin Griffin pointed to their popularity: 'There was a tremendous interest in prayer at that time after Vatican II.' Fr Hurley has compiled the list of topics, speakers and dates for all of the 146 lectures. Jesuits gave 116 of them, with four by Dublin diocesan priests – John M. Nolan of UCD twice, Feichín O'Doherty, also UCD, and Liam Breen, a curate – and nine by lay men and women.[23]

Glenstal Liturgical Congresses

Liturgical congresses were organised annually for 21 years by the Benedictine monks at Glenstal, Co Limerick, before, during and after the Council, with a large attendance of clergy and some laity. Fr Griffin adds this to Canon McGarry and Fr Flannery as the third factor which 'saved the Irish church'. Archbishop McQuaid probably had reservations, as indicated when Fr Burke Savage, in 1965, submitted a list of proposed lecturers for a Unity Week series and Dom Joseph Dowdall, Abbot of Glenstal, was one of the names rejected.[24]

Dublin Diocesan Outreach programme

From the 1950s there was an annual programme of lectures for adults, in co-ordination with adult education boards and vocational education committees throughout the archdiocese. Liberal-minded theologians such as Fr Seán Fagan, a Marist priest, and Fr Hurley were on the panel of lecturers. Lay volunteers, usually members of the lay order, Knights of St Columbanus, drove the lecturers to the schools.[25] Fr Hurley says the lectures were an initiative of Mgr Tom Fehily, Director of the Dublin Institute of Catholic Sociology, with the encouragement of Archbishop McQuaid: 'He certainly knew about them and allowed them.' Fr Fagan admires McQuaid's concern for adult education, with lay involvement, 'because he used lay groups and there was little in the way of funding, nothing at all. The drivers and lecturers gave their services free.' It was clear that McQuaid wanted the laity to be educated about the Council, but some of the older priests were not so supportive. The outreach lectures continued through and after the Council. The programme for 1965/66, for example, included numerous updates on the Council and there were several lay lecturers.[26] Fr Liam Breen, treasurer, told McQuaid that in the 1966 season there were 136 lectures, covering 121 centres with an average attendance of 20 and very good discussion.[27]

Patrician Year

The 1500th anniversary of the death of St Patrick was celebrated in 1961. National ceremonies were held in Armagh, in March, with James Cardinal McIntyre as Papal Delegate. In June, Archbishop McQuaid held a week-long Patrician Congress in Dublin, also favoured with a Papal Delegate, Gregory Cardinal Agagianian, and culminating with Mass in Croke Park before as big an attendance as there ever was at a gaelic football or hurling match there. McQuaid and Agagianian were driven around the ground in an open-top limousine blessing the cheering crowd. There is evidence that the two men did not like each other. Auxiliary Bishop Patrick Dunne wrote to McQuaid: 'They say that Cardinal Agagianian is somewhat inscrutable, incommunicative, but always charming. But Your Grace's labour will not be lightened by his coming.' McQuaid's note: 'Thank you. I never sought the honour. Honour it is, but a great worry.'[28]

Mgr Fehily was Congress Director, and it is still remembered for the Congress Volunteer Corps, a group of schoolboys who were brought together for stewarding duties. Archbishop Diarmuid Martin was one of them. Mgr Fehily says there were two hundred of them in uniform and when it was decided to disband them after the Congress, the Taoiseach, Seán Lemass, urged McQuaid to keep them on because there was no youth movement of that calibre of education. They have remained as a social work organisation now known as the Colleges Volunteer Corps.

John Feeney considered the Congress as a 'glittering bejewelled spectacle of Catholic life just before the Council', before the realities of the church impinged too strongly on Ireland.[29] Fergal Tobin regarded it as 'the most public manifestation' of Dublin's Catholicism since the Eucharistic Congress of 1932, noting that no Protestant churchmen were invited to participate in any of the events.[30] Deirdre McMahon saw it as 'the apotheosis' of McQuaid's episcopate and of 'the Tridentine, post-Cullenite church in which he had lived most of his life'.[31]

Radharc television documentaries

Archbishop McQuaid agreed in March 1959 to send two Dublin priests, Fr Joe Dunn and Fr Desmond Forristal, to a television course in Manchester, run by Fr Agnellus Andrew for ABC (TV), and taken by all BBC producers. Only Fr Dunn was accepted as places were limited.[32] Cathal Canon McCarthy, President, Clonliffe College, and McQuaid's adviser on broadcasting, then heard from Mgr Fehily at DICS about a course for Radio and TV at the Academy of Broadcasting Arts, New York, and wrote to Fr Liam Martin, the Archbishop's secretary: 'I do think that we have no time to spare in equipping a priest or better two priests for television.'[33] McQuaid acted promptly, sending Fr Dunn and Fr Forristal on the three-month course and paying their expenses. When McQuaid received their report he noted: 'Thank you. What I sought. Clear, well-ordered, completed, 25/1/60.'[34]

This led to the Radharc television film unit, which made documentaries on religious and social topics in Ireland and around the world. They sold their work to the newly-established Irish television station, Telefís Éireann, now RTÉ, and they made 400 films in 35 years, the longest-running programme of its type in the history of the station.

The late Fr Dunn has written his account of Radharc.[35] Whether it was McQuaid himself, or Canon McCarthy, or Fr Dunn, or Mgr Fehily, who first had the idea, the archbishop encouraged it, continued to release priests to it and did not interfere with topics or content of programmes. He did not control it but ultimately he could have effectively finished it by withdrawing his priests, but he did not. The correspondence reflects well on him.

Fr Dunn told him:

Two days before Your Grace returned from Rome, our little programme 'Radharc' received the Jacobs Award for most enterprising programme on Telefís Éireann in competition with *Broadsheet* and the *Late Late Show*. Roughly 400,000 people now watch each programme.

McQuaid noted this, telling Fr Dunn that Radharc was now a Dublin unit, independent of TÉ, of the Central Catholic Advisory Committee and of Fr Romuald Dodd OP, Director of Religious Programmes, but 'subject to me and in religious matters to my liaison officer, Canon McCarthy. Gave £500 for an editing machine.'

Fr Dunn told McQuaid there were long delays before terms were agreed for the coming season, partly because of TÉ's 'obvious anxiety that we work through Fr Dodd, and my determination not to'. McQuaid congratulated him on his stand and told him 'to stand clear from Father Dodd OP. You are not a "religious" programme, and you are subject directly to me in your work'.[36]

But things were to change. By 1970, Radharc was nearly completely run by lay people, with Fr Forristal and Fr Dermod McCarthy the only priests remaining. Fr Dunn was now in charge of the Communications Centre, as well as the new Catholic Communications Institute, of which it was a part, working under Archbishop Morris of Cashel & Emly. Radharc had an influential critic in Mgr Cecil Barrett and McQuaid's enthusiasm was diminishing. Mgr Barrett wrote to McQuaid in late 1969 fearing that Radharc might suffer from Fr Dunn being so involved in his new appointment:

> Recent Radharc programmes have not been so impressive. They may have been excellent technically, but this isn't enough. They must not drift away from their primary purpose, viz to publicise the church in a positive manner.[37]

Mgr Barrett felt 'both Radharc and the Communications Centre are going to suffer if Father Dunn has to pull out … They [Dunn and Morris] seem to be drifting without a compass; if they are not careful, they will find themselves on the Rocks.'[38] McQuaid informed Fr Dunn of Mgr Barrett's criticism of the programme, *Eggs in the Hay*, on popular Irish superstitions, and Fr Dunn did not defend it:

> It would be wrong for me to disclaim responsibility for last Sunday's programme and I won't therefore attempt it. I didn't like the programme much either … In the memorandum which I sent to Your Grace last Sunday, I gave as one of the reasons for perhaps giving Father Forristal more completely to the operation of Radharc would be 'to exercise a more effective control over Father McCarthy and the two lay editors'. Earlier on the same page I refer more explicitly to lack of judgement.[39]

Nine months later, the archbishop removed Fr McCarthy from Radharc and appointed him to Athy parish as curate. Fr McCarthy says he did not know about Mgr Barrett's and Fr Dunn's criticism of the superstitions programme but had believed it was two programmes on nuns that had caused McQuaid to move him. Fr McCarthy says the programmes on the position of nuns after Vatican II, made with Fr John Wall, who was also moved to another parish soon afterwards, showed that the reforms were not being implemented and that nuns felt greatly frustrated. Mgr Barrett, parish priest in Booterstown, the parish where the Radharc unit was based, intervened with the sister principal of a local convent school after he heard that shooting for the programmes had started and had been done, with her permission, in her school. The Radharc people were 'thrown out' and they eventually made the programmes with other religious-run schools in different parishes and dioceses.

Fr McCarthy praises Radharc as 'one of the most enlightened initiatives of John Charles' time ... And he didn't think it would work, but he was prepared to go along with it ...' When Fr McCarthy was moved to Athy, Fr Forristal asked McQuaid to reconsider the appointment, saying he would now be the only priest regularly in Radharc and that Fr McCarthy's move would make 'things difficult for the time being'. The reply was that it would not be possible 'to change, or postpone' Fr McCarthy's appointment, adding, 'from your description of his work, there would seem to be nothing in it that calls for the presence of a priest'. Fr Dunn replied that he 'naturally' regretted the loss of another priest in a relatively short period.[40]

Mgr Tom Stack, once a member of the team, says 'Radharc was able to, in a subtle way and perhaps not even totally consciously, say things to the Irish church about the Irish church through the medium of the churches abroad ...'. Others also praise John Charles for the Radharc initiative: Cardinal Connell: '... a man of great foresight'; Patrick Masterson: '... and these people, they were not safe men; Joe Dunn was a very independent spirit'; Seán MacRéamoinn: '... ahead of any of his colleagues'; John Horgan: 'the richness of the Radharc heritage is unbelievable'; Bishop Murray: '... He saw that television was coming and you had to be up there ...'; Michael Gill: '... one of the great, good influences where he [McQuaid] was forward and looking ahead'; Fr Eltin Griffin: '… a big plus for him'; Mgr MacMahon: '… a very positive development …'; Elizabeth Lovatt-Dolan: 'Radharc opened all kinds of doors to all kinds of people … opening windows, because we were very enclosed and we were very much into the model of the church triumphant …'.

The archbishop's encouragement and financial support in the early days of Radharc was appreciated, and he released priests to work with Fr Dunn and Fr Forristal, but these priests were appointed by Radharc and responsible to Radharc for their work in film. There was some concern, however, about legal responsibilities and potential litigation against the diocese. Radharc agreed to indemnify RTÉ against any claims but the diocese does not seem to have done anything to formalise the matter nor to indemnify itself. However, Radharc soon began to take on a life of its own with Joe Dunn and Des Forristal registering it as a business name in 1964. Joe maintained with RTÉ that Radharc was owned and operated by himself and Des. Any money lent by the diocese in the early days was repaid in full out of sales of their programmes to RTÉ. Legal advisers eventually concluded that Radharc was a partnership owned by the two priests although a partnership deed as such cannot be found.[41] Des Forristal retired from the partnership in 1981 and finally, in January 1984, with the co-operation of the Revenue Commissioners, it was turned into a charitable trust with Joe Dunn and his brother, Peter, as trustees. Joe Dunn dealt briefly with this matter himself and also asserted that he had no record or memory of interference by McQuaid or his successors.[42]

CHAPTER THREE

From Dream to Reality –
The Council Meets

The bishops, in full ecclesiastical dress, met in Rome in the autumns of 1962, 1963, 1964 and 1965. They came from all parts of the world and displayed their differences on theological questions in a direct manner which took many people by surprise. Archbishop John Charles McQuaid was seen as very diligent, but shocked by what was happening, never at ease with it, and then accepting it as the work of the Holy Spirit within the church and voting in favour of the final documents. The media were seen not to have made the Council into an issue but to have moved it along, with the co-operation of liberal bishops and their advisers, forcing a new transparency and accountability in the central governing authority of the church, which eventually percolated to local level.

McQuaid's expectation at the start of the Council in autumn 1962 was consistent with the 'no change' message that he brought home at the end, and with his views on ecumenism. He hoped, in a letter to his priests, that

> ... The Faithful will be careful not to expect from the Council what in the plan of God it is not meant to achieve. They will guard against undue expectation of new definitions of doctrine, new laws of discipline, new or startling movements towards the unity of Christendom ... We hope that God, in his mercy, may incline the hearts of those who live separated from us in doctrine and discipline to turn towards the only Truth ... If it should please the Council to issue new laws concerning the discipline of Catholic life, we will accept the decrees and loyally execute the commands of the Holy Father and the Council.[1]

Irish bishops at the Council

The first session, October-December 1962, established patterns for the remaining three sessions, with bishops rejecting the Roman Curia's selections of chairmen for the meetings and amending, even rejecting, documents presented by the Curia for discussion. Many views of these bishops were adopted finally as majority views. Archbishop McQuaid tended to be sympathetic to curial viewpoints. He was most active in the First Session, leading the Irish bishops, because John Cardinal D'Alton, Chairman of the Irish Episcopal Conference, was terminally ill. McQuaid made two of his three contributions to the Council debates during the first session. Cardinal D'Alton died in February 1963 and William Conway, his successor as Archbishop of Armagh, was chairman for the remaining sessions.

McQuaid agreed to a meeting of Irish bishops with their English and Scottish counterparts, at which Cardinal Godfrey of Westminster said the purpose was 'to suggest means by which the business of the Council could be accelerated'. A sub-committee, with McQuaid as chairman, and a further meeting, led to an agreed proposal, influenced by Bishop Browne of Galway, calling for even greater media secrecy. It requested a drastic reduction of *schemata*, so as 'to present to the Fathers only what is of vital interest to the Council'. The Irish hierarchy agreed to continue consultation and collaboration. McQuaid seems to have dominated these proceedings and studied the documentation with his usual diligence. Agreed points were sent to Cardinal Cicognani, Secretary of State, for the Council's consideration. McQuaid told Cardinal McIntyre of Los Angeles that the Irish bishops would retain their independent position, while maintaining contact with the British hierarchy.[2]

On return to Dublin, Archbishop McQuaid, in early 1963, suggested a series of expert lectures for the bishops, but there was opposition. The lectures were postponed and did not take place. However, he asked Jesuits Frs Kevin Smyth and M. A. O'Grady, two of the proposed lecturers, to help him personally by preparing exactly what he had asked: 'Your papers will be of great benefit to me when the *schemata* come back to me in a few weeks. I shall, I hope, see you both again'.[3]

Fr Smyth was to prepare an outline of Middle European

theology. This indicates that McQuaid wished to take advice on Council issues before replying to Rome and he was trying to understand trends in Europe and the work of Frs Karl Rahner, Hans Küng and others, which were a source of controversy at the First Session. Also, he probably realised that the other Irish bishops were not well-informed.

The Irish hierarchy met together in Rome during the Council sessions. A committee to discuss the 'problem' of the vernacular [local languages instead of Latin] in the Liturgy reported in November 1963 that they were reluctant to change and would prefer only to do so if they had to. It proposed they all move together on changes and maintain uniformity throughout the country. It seemed to them that the proposed *Constitution on the Sacred Liturgy* imposed no 'juridical obligation' to introduce the vernacular, '… if left to ourselves, we would in all probability prefer the *status quo*'. They made a case to hold out against the vernacular until all of the reforms were complete, rather than have piecemeal changes over a period of years which 'will tend to confuse the ordinary faithful and dispose them to regard nothing in faith, morals, or discipline as outside the possibility of change'.[4]

One priest recalls his 'excitement' as a student in Rome during the Council, attending meetings with journalists and liberal bishops and theologians who had become media celebrities. The archbishop never enquired but this priest thinks he 'disapproved immensely of all this stuff'. John Horgan says Irish diocesan bishops were 'not great mixers' at the Council and seemed to go straight back to the Irish College after the day's debates. Fr Eltin Griffin says the Irish bishops were taken by surprise at the Council, that 'they hadn't a clue' and sent for Fr Cahal Daly, not then a bishop, 'to enlighten them'.

The government was interested. During the second session, in November 1963, Hugh McCann, Secretary, Department of External Affairs, wrote to Tommy Commins, Irish Ambassador to the Holy See, that the Minister [Frank Aiken]

has indicated a wish to have any available information about what is happening at the current session of the Ecumenical Council and, in particular, the general attitude of the Irish bishops and the main problems. I understand that the

President [Éamon de Valera] and others have been talking to him in the matter.[5]

Commins reported back that the Irish bishops 'taken as a body or individually, with one or two notable exceptions, are a completely closed book'. He said that even in relaxed gatherings like lunch 'they are not forthcoming in any positive way in expressing constructive views on the matters being dealt with in the Council ...'

Commins' next paragraph, 'top secret', says

Even the Irish *Periti* [theological advisers] such as, e.g. Msgr Herlihy and Father Cremin who are in day to day and, indeed, one might say, hour to hour contact with the bishops and on whose expertise the bishops one would think would be anxious to draw, are I know never consulted by the body of bishops and are not in fact permitted to be present at any meetings which the bishops hold in the Irish College for the discussion of Council matters.[6]

Commins said this 'reflects an oyster-like and thus far completely impenetrable characteristic of the Irish hierarchy' adding that

it has always been evident that their whole attitude to the Council itself has been the reverse of exuberant and the only thing which one can deduce with certainty from contact with them, is that their first reaction to any given problem within the Council will be supremely conservative. A notable exception, and as far as I can see, the only one, is Bishop Philbin of Down and Connor ...[7]

Commins reported, 'highly confidential', in July 1964, that there was 'little indication' that the [Irish] hierarchy as a body or as individuals, had moved from the 'rather supine and reserved approach to the Council and Council problems which has characterised their participation in the last two sessions'.[8]

Preparing responses to Tim Pat Coogan's queries in 1965, which Coogan did not receive, as to whether the Irish people were impressed or unimpressed with the showing or contribution of the hierarchy at the Council, McQuaid, with Mgr MacMahon and Osmond Dowling, said it was 'difficult to say' short of something like a survey. Some of the books on the Council had attempted an estimate, but it was 'hard to say how far they influenced public opinion'. And, in (apparently) Dowling's handwriting:

> It would be quite wrong to suggest that the Council was composed of rival hierarchies engaged in capping one another's contributions, but in fact the quality of the scholastic and theological thought brought to the Council reflected great credit on this country.

Archbishop Morris of Cashel & Emly, in a 1992 interview, sensitive portions of which were published only after his death, recalled that he had been a bishop for two years when the Council started and was 'quite insular' in his outlook on the church and his theology. He 'didn't know what sort of issues were likely to come up in Rome' but that he had heard of a pastoral letter issued by the bishops of Holland. Archbishop McQuaid had told him about it, regarding it as 'too advanced, unorthodox', but he himself 'didn't know about the cleavages within the theology schools'.[10]

Archbishop McQuaid at the Council

Mgr Ardle MacMahon and Mgr Michael O'Connell were Archbishop McQuaid's secretaries at the Council. Mgr MacMahon confirms that the Archbishop was present at all of the debates and kept in closest touch with the English, Australian and New Zealand hierarchies. He says McQuaid never discussed with him 'what one might call the *übeblick*, or the overview of the Council as such; maybe, some individual parts, but not the whole lot'. Mgr Tom Fehily was in Rome for one week during the second session, 'for the experience', and he recalls that the archbishop 'examined the texts very carefully. He spent all his time in the evenings studying them.'

McQuaid was aware of his low profile at the Council and told Fr Burke Savage in 1966: 'I lived as a hermit in Rome ...'[11] Correspondence shows, however, that he met other bishops and moved about more than has been supposed. He received many invitations to functions, most of which he turned down, preferring those that were directly related to the Council rather than social events.[12]

He had an intriguing correspondence from 'Karel', a young priest working in the Roman Curia, who wrote him a postcard, dated 13 November 1962, with the typed heading 'Segretaria di Stato, di sua santita', crossed out. Karel wrote: 'Father Nouven [Newman?], Thomas More and I are so grateful for Your Grace's extreme kindness to us. How much of Your precious time was given to us just [?] how we appreciate it. Thomas says he believes nobody could value more highly than we do Your Grace's goodness to us. We just humbly pray for all of Your Grace's intentions as a little way of reciprocating. And I myself know it is a privilege every morning to see Your Grace again, who among all the other Fathers (besides my own Cardinal) is for me the one who has given me most with respect to enriching my priesthood. Your Grace's humble son Karel.' There was further correspondence, 27 November 1962, when Karel wrote, this time from 'Pontificia Accademe Ecclesiastica' – to where he had apparently moved from the Secretariat of State: 'These days I have been using, thanks to Your Grace's truly paternal generosity, the book *Intima Divina*. I first thought it was rather like the others, but I now feel (another proof of my humility being ever so slow, slow, slow) it is helping me a great deal. Your Grace's care and affection which nobody – I venture to say it – could treasure more, only enhances my filial love and devotion for Ireland's Primate.' McQuaid had a habit of giving people presents of spiritual books. He had sent Karel a copy of P. Gabriel's *Intimité Divina*, 2 vols. There is a docket in the files, dated December 1965, for 6,700 lire, for his order of another copy from a Rome bookshop.[13]

Interviewees have referred to John Charles' pleasure at the precedence he was given, as Archbishop of Dublin, in the Council seating arrangements. He was described as 'Primas I' and seated next to the cardinals because he was the senior primate of a country. Mgr MacMahon says this 'made it nice for him'; John Brophy believes he saw it as the next best thing to being a cardinal. He later showed Vincent Gallagher a bound volume of the Council proceedings where he was listed, 'the first metropolitan of the universal church, the leading primate'.

Louis McRedmond believes McQuaid became more and more isolated because of the consistency of his views, which were unpopular and seen as supporting the curial minority. He admires him for this consistency, while not agreeing with him, and compares him favourably against some of the other Irish bishops.

What Archbishop McQuaid said at the Council

Two of McQuaid's interventions, on behalf of the Irish hierarchy, were on the liturgy, during the first session, 24 and 30 October 1962. He surrendered his right to speak on the church, 7 November 1962. His intervention in the ecumenism debate, during the second session, 19 November 1963, was on his own behalf. Mgr MacMahon says his contributions to the debates were 'brief and to the point, and in very good Latin'. The archives contain handwritten drafts of some of these interventions and written submissions on matters circulated to the bishops between sessions. He studied every document and circular with care and was meticulous in the wording of his submissions.

Constitution on the Sacred Liturgy

Archbishop McQuaid's address, 24 October 1962, on Chapter 1 of the liturgy document was a mere 97 words. He referred to Pope Pius XII's encyclical *Mediator Dei* (1947) and its emphasis on the active participation of the people in the Mass and on the Mass as a sacrifice, and suggested that all of the Irish bishops wanted an added paragraph to this effect.[14] Xavier Rynne reported McQuaid saying he wanted the Latin language retained in the Mass but could see the utility of allowing the vernacular in the administration of the sacraments. There is no reference in the published version to Latin or the vernacular.

McQuaid spoke again on behalf of the Irish bishops, 30 October 1962, on Chapter 2 of the liturgy document. In the course of his 214 words, he said that 'pastors of souls should take care that the faithful acknowledge the sacrifice of the Mass as the centre of their religious life'. The Irish bishops were not in favour of communion under both species of bread and wine, even in special cases, and they preferred the Tridentine discipline to be 'religiously observed'. On the question of extending the practice of concelebrated Masses, the Irish bishops 'are of the opinion that the reason which would make desirable its extension is not verified in our country'. They believed the people were happier having several Masses celebrated at the one time on different altars.[16]

Bishop Edward Joyce, of Christchurch, New Zealand, rang Archbishop McQuaid at the Irish College after this address and Mgr MacMahon, who took the call in his absence, wrote him a note that Bishop Joyce said a number of the Fathers had spoken to him

> of Your Grace's intervention in the discussion on Chapter 2 of the liturgical scheme today. Cardinal Gilroy [Australia] was very pleased, considering the presentation clear and concise, and he would fully agree with the content. Cardinal D'Alton has spoken highly of the intervention.[17]

Rynne refers to some speakers that day being against innovation in the liturgy, while others were favourable to the *schema* generally but felt there was room for certain modifications and reservations. He adds that 'Archbishop McQuaid of Dublin came out once more against any thought of change', but does not make it clear that he was speaking on behalf of the Irish hierarchy.[18] That sentence and the words 'once more' would seem unfair to the archbishop.

Decree on Ecumenism

McQuaid's address to the Council on the ecumenism document is a brief 118 words in the concise Latin version. He said:

> The document on ecumenism is in general acceptable; insofar as sound doctrine is concerned there are many matters extremely well expressed.
> I should, however, like, with due respect, to add just this.
> Experience has shown that very many, including highly educated Catholics, tend to confuse certain sincere, benevolent expressions on the part of non-Catholics in relation to the church with an intention of mind and heart of accepting the entire doctrine of the church.
> We bishops, however, long versed over many years in dealing with newly converted non-Catholics, have learned from experience rather than books. We have discovered that converts who accept the Catholic faith wish, in the last analy-

sis, to understand specifically the Catholic doctrine set out, not nebulously but precisely, a doctrine that is not simply the speculations of private theologians, but as set out in serene and pastoral terms by the Holy Roman See.[19]

There is also a more critical written submission from McQuaid on a draft of Chapter 2, par 7 of the *Decree on Ecumenism*. It was possibly a response to a Curia request for comments. It is very critical of certain new ecumenical approaches:

> It is clear that simple Faithful who were brought up on the old catechesis, and abhorred heresy from their infancy, would find it very difficult, if not impossible to understand how today it could be possible to have common prayer with heretics ...

In another extract from the same submission, McQuaid believes 'It would require a very lengthy process of preparation to prevent scandal and even damage to the Faith arising.'[20]

He also expressed to Mgr Dino Staffa in the Curia, 6 October 1964, his concern about the ecumenism decree. This was clearly submitted in response to a circulated document. Chapter 2, paragraph 8 was a 'grave worry': 'It is altogether repugnant to me.' This paragraph in the final document refers to common prayer and, on special occasions, common worship with non-Catholics. He wanted the entire paragraph changed so that it would be clearly explained to the Faithful how such sharing could be lawful in relation to their [non-Catholics] presence at the administration and reception of the sacraments.[21]

One interpretation of the Staffa letter was that McQuaid 'disagreed in principle' with the draft text.[22] That does not seem to have been so, as shown in his formal address to the Council, but he opposed those parts which seemed to go against all of his nature, especially the matter of joint prayer services with Protestants. His bewilderment was expressed earlier to Fr Burke Savage: 'I suppose we may as well close down the Catholic Enquiry Centre, since Protestants "do not need to be converted to God in Christ".'[23]

Dogmatic Constitution on the Church

McQuaid ceded his place as a speaker on Chapter 4 of the document on the church, 7 November 1962, and left it as a written submission, an *animadversio scripta*, which amounts to 276 words. This chapter refers to the vocation to sanctity in the church. McQuaid was keen to stress that the church was not just the clergy and those in religious orders and congregations but the entire membership. All were equally called to sanctity and it was possible for them to achieve it – fathers, mothers, families.[24]

Declaration on Religious Freedom

McQuaid did not contribute publicly to debates about the document on religious freedom but his undated notes show he feared 'inevitable misunderstandings especially among the ordinary Faithful' and commented that

> more emphasis should be placed on the rights of God the creator. The *schema* is chiefly concerned with the so-called rights of the creature. Right cannot be based on the private judgement of individuals. Erroneous conscience confers no right to perform what it commands.[25]

In another undated document, he commented on specific sections of the religious freedom draft. He believed that the words 'except when the exercise of religion might injure public order' might '*prima facie*' be understood by communist states 'to their own advantage to justify coercive action against the Catholic religion'. He suggested the text be rephrased so that the implications of the words 'public order' and particularly the 'common good' be more clear and he added: 'The exercise of true religion can in no way injure the objective common good.' He accepted that the document seemed founded on human dignity, but 'human dignity as a current expression is far from clear and requires to be explained'. He suggested the text be amplified 'so as to demonstrate that human dignity is founded on the excellence of man in relation to created things as well as on the Natural Law and an intelligence and will as well as being derived from Divine Grace'.[26]

Early Council documents

The *Constitution on the Sacred Liturgy* was the first document of the Council. During Archbishop McQuaid's years, its effects were the most visible because of changes in the Mass, sacraments and other liturgical matters. The *Decree on Ecumenism*, the *Dogmatic Constitution on the Church* and the *Pastoral Constitution on the Church in the Modern World* also drew special attention, but some of the other documents did not have such immediate effect.

Changes in the Mass, effectively the first since the Council of Trent in the sixteenth century, were gradual, but everybody could soon see that the Mass was now spoken in their local language, the vernacular. Bishop Donal Murray says liturgical change developed its own momentum, going further than the Council had decided. The Council said the place of Latin was to be kept 'and they never assumed that the whole of the Mass would be in the vernacular'. Archbishop McQuaid did not disguise how he felt, especially about some of the changes in the Mass. He defended his position to the Public Image Committee:

> In dealing with the modern call for a more pastoral liturgy, we should remember that our grandparents were able to know exactly what the Mass meant from the *Key of Heaven* where they had the Latin Ordinary of the Mass and an English translation, or prayers based on the Ordinary.[27]

He wrote a pastoral letter in full support of the Council document and asked people to rejoice in it:

> Forgotten now the words of controversy, the moments of tension when in our anxiety to be faithful to our sacred trust, each had striven in his human way, but with earnest faith, to formulate true teaching that would benefit the church.

He was pleased that greater emphasis was to be given to the liturgy in seminary training, 'not merely rubrics and ceremonies but the doctrine, history and spiritual application of the liturgy'. Not all, however, would change 'but only that of which the change will promote the dignity of God's worship and make the meaning of that worship more easy to understand'.[28] He continued to say his own private Mass in Latin, as it was still optional, suggesting to Fr Lehane: '... isn't it much nicer?' He was in agreement with Papal Nuncio Sensi's letter in 1965 that the Holy See was concerned about the 'falling off in the standard of Latin studies in seminaries and other houses of formation for clerical students'. In reply, he regretted that

> ... we are approaching a position in which the clergy can no longer be regarded as a learned body in the old sense. And nothing can halt the progress ... I have very firmly resisted the tendency to disregard the learning and the use of Latin.[29]

Canon Battelle remembers 'the main thing about John Charles was that he had a tremendous respect for the Eucharist', but his views were under strain. Mgr Stephen Greene says he did not want the Mass to be interpreted solely as a meal, 'he was very keen on the emphasis on the sacrifice'. Mgr Greene was a diocesan censor of religious publications and was told to watch out for this point, McQuaid's secretary, Mgr Michael O'Connell, giving him the 'mind' of the archbishop that 'if any article came through that would reduce the Mass to being just a meal, even if you called it a sacred meal, that it was to be ostracised'. Mgr Tom Fehily says McQuaid saw a problem in the Protestant churches regarding the Eucharist as a meal while 'we regard it as a sacrifice, not a meal'.

Archbishop McQuaid provided new churches and schools as Dublin city spread into the suburbs and new housing estates, but he was often criticised for building large churches of poor design. He defended himself to the Public Image Committee:

> His Grace had been accused of building completely drab churches. He has in fact left every parish priest free to choose the architect and the design. The present Pope [Paul VI, on a visit in 1961] went around with His Grace to all the new churches in Dublin and examined them very closely. He commented 'these are lovely churches' and 'certainly you know them to be churches'.[30]

He came to terms with changes in architecture and interior church design, especially the replacement of the traditional high altar by a small table-like structure closer to the people. In both cases he was more supportive of the changes than was generally believed. Fr Seán Fagan was superior of the Marist Fathers community in Milltown in 1963: 'I was re-doing the chapel and we moved the marble altar out from the back wall to have Mass facing the people'. He said nothing about it to the archbishop as it was a private oratory and not a public chapel. At the same time, they built a large extension to their House of Studies and McQuaid came to bless it. Fr Fagan says: 'I didn't celebrate the Mass from behind, facing the people, as I thought it would embarrass him.' So, he said the Mass in front of the altar in the old way. McQuaid never made a single reference to the new altar, but two weeks later, a parish priest called and said the archbishop had sent him out to have a look at the chapel. Soon after, another parish priest came with the same message. 'And yet John Charles never said a word about it to me,' Fr Fagan recalls, but 'he told these priests, who were looking for permission to refurbish their church, to go and look at ours in Milltown ... He was impressed by it.' Canon Battelle says McQuaid had difficulty with the idea of the priest facing the people, was slow on the removal of the traditional altar-rails, and used to 'cringe' at Lourdes when he saw portable altars being wheeled out in front of the permanent ones.

Vincent Gallagher was architect for two later churches, Our Lady Seat of Wisdom, Belfield (UCD) and the parish church of Our Lady of Dolours, Glasnevin. He says McQuaid 'was very impressed' and 'very pleased' when he came up with an octagonal church for Belfield that was post-Vatican II in design. The altar was free-standing and the tabernacle on a dais, or pedestal, behind it. When the sanctuary was designed Gallagher asked McQuaid if he wanted altar-rails. The written reply: 'Dear Mr Gallagher, in Dublin, we all kneel.' When the design for the Glasnevin church was ready, he says McQuaid was so pleased that he said to the priests with him: 'Oh, by Jove, Fathers, have a look at this here.' He later told him: 'You know, Vincent, what would others think about us now when we build this church?'

The Legion of Mary at the Council

McQuaid favoured the Legion of Mary, an association of Catholic lay people, organised on the model of an army, and founded in 1921 by Frank Duff (1889-1980), another past pupil of Blackrock College. Vincent Gallagher remembers his 'respect and awe' for Duff and his sanctity. At this time, the Legion claimed an active membership of nearly one and a half million worldwide and nine million auxiliary members, but Duff was 'uncomfortable' that the Council and its aftermath seemed to involve a swing away from mariology. He was against those who suggested the Legion needed updating and change.[31] It has been suggested that it was not until the 1960s that Frank Duff felt the Legion enjoyed the Archbishop's 'full support'.[32] Maurice Hartigan refers to the Legion's early impact on the prostitution issue in Dublin and the feeling that it was encroaching on the priestly ministry. This aroused hostility from the previous archbishop, Edward Byrne, and other senior churchmen, in particular, between 1927 and 1935.[33]

While McQuaid set up a *praesidium* [branch] of the Legion with the final year boys in Blackrock College in 1939,[34] and saw the Legion as 'a crucial force in creating a socially-minded Catholicism',[35] there was an unease in his relationship with them after 1944 when he suppressed the Mercier Society for dialogue with Protestants, in which Frank Duff and other legionaries were prominent. Fr Michael O'Carroll regarded this, and the similar suppression of The Pillar of Fire Society for dialogue with Jews, as serious mistakes by McQuaid.[36]

There was speculation that the role of Mary and the Legion might be under fire at the later stages of the Council, but McQuaid assured Duff he would be there to carry on the fight for them. Duff wrote to him: 'We must all be happy at the providential turn which took place at the end of the last session in regard to Our Blessed Lady.' Some had wanted a separate document about Mary, but the Council Fathers included the topic in the *Dogmatic Constitution on the Church*. Duff made reference to a Cardinal Suenens letter:

> He is apparently completely satisfied about *De Ecclesia* [the Constitution] and Our Lady. You will notice his postscript about her and apostleship. Truly the campaign of the minimisers has boomeranged on themselves but they have been very successful in shaking the faith of many over the continent of Europe ...[37]

McQuaid replied that he did not know what the Cardinal meant by 'the Legion in the next session' but 'please God, I will be there and if the Legion comes up, I must be reckoned with'.[38]

Even after some disappointments, he still had fight left in him for the 'minimisers', or, we presume, the 'liberals'. Leon-Joseph Cardinal Suenens, Archbishop of Malines-Brussels, was a prominent and popular liberal at the Council, and a public champion of the Legion. He was a regular visitor to Ireland. Frank Duff continued his lobby for the Legion, writing to Pope Paul VI, who replied through Cardinal Cicognani, Secretary of State, with 'praise and encouragement to the Legion of Mary, which, first born in the mystic climate of Catholic Ireland, has by now extended its beneficent action to every continent'.[39] Duff passed this letter to McQuaid, who hoped that the Pope's 'patronage' would assist areas 'where bishops have not found space for the Legion'.[40]

Media during the Council
The opening of the Council, in October 1962, received prominent coverage in the Irish newspapers. Seán Cryan was there for the *Irish Press* and Liam Shine for the *Irish Independent*. *The Irish Times* did not have a staff reporter there but coverage was by Michael Wall and news agencies. Headlines, all on Page 1, were: 'Vatican Council Opens' (*Irish Press*, 12/10/62); 'Epochal Rome Event' (*Irish Independent* 12/10/62); 'Pope and People Rejoice' (*The Irish Times* 12/10/62). The ceremonial splendour, with photographs and the Pope's address, were featured, as well as the evening torchlight procession. Cardinal D'Alton's message to the Irish people and the celebration of his 80th birthday was also prominent. After the opening, all took their reports from agencies, while RTÉ had Seán MacRéamoinn and Kevin O'Kelly reporting and commenting at various stages. It was not until the final session, autumn 1965, that Irish newspaper staff journalists and commentators, Louis McRedmond, *Irish Independent* and John Horgan, *The Irish Times*, attended. Desmond Fisher represented *The Catholic Herald* of London.

Journalists had difficulty getting information out of the Council. The debates were in Latin and not open to the press and the daily press releases were, at first, a list of speakers with a bland translated précis, without attribution, of what was said. The first session was worst in this regard, but procedures eased somewhat subsequently.

Louis McRedmond said journalists at the first session

> ... were deliberately thrown back on second-rate and third-rate sources ... Of course the reports, *qua* reports, merited censure. But where did the major fault lie? It was indeed a classic example of the church's lack of understanding of the simple rule of evidence by which every reporter is bound ...[41]

McRedmond received a 'shattering jolt' on return to Ireland at the end of the Council. There was 'confusion and misconception, disappointment and misplaced enthusiasm; scarcely an attitude could be found which coincided with what the journalist had known in the shadow of St Peter's. It was humbling at first. Had I and my colleagues somehow fallen down on the job?'[42] John Horgan has related a similar experience of how 'astonishing and frustrating' it was to discover that 'all the theological, historical and liturgical richness to which we had been exposed in Rome, and which had left an indelible mark on all who experienced it, had only touched the fringes of Irish Catholicism'.[43]

Archbishop McQuaid was remote from the media at the Council. Seán MacRéamoinn never met him in Rome and John Horgan doesn't recall ever talking to him there. Louis McRedmond had one meeting with him and, when he enquired at the Irish College for reactions, he was usually put on to Mgr Ardle MacMahon or Mgr Frank Cremin.

McQuaid remained critical of the media coverage and when members of the Public Image Committee expressed alarm at the rise of criticism about church and bishops, he said:

> I don't think we should be alarmed at the present climate. It was there, it always was, the Vatican Council has lifted it. The criticism produced is quite ignorant, the reporting on the Council has been very bad – deplorable. Even Schillebeeckx is inaccurate. If he, why not Desmond Fisher whose reporting I thought very objectionable. So how can you blame the people? But I should not be alarmed – just as I would not be alarmed at current press campaign. These are things I dare not say outside this room.[44]

He told Fr Burke Savage, from Rome: 'I am dismayed by the facile ignorance of the journalists who are writing about the documents that have cost us years of work, and by the more facile dictation in regard to what we bishops must now do.'[45] Louis McRedmond remembers McQuaid telling him: 'You know, Mr McRedmond, when I read the newspapers, I wonder are these people at the same Council as I am.' In McRedmond's view, McQuaid felt the Council was being misrepresented in the way it was being publicised and he was referring to the more liberal journalists and writers.

The Dominican priest, Ambrose McNicholl, seemed to understand this reasonable dilemma of McQuaid, and many others, when he said a bishop would not see things the same way as a *peritus*, nor a member of a conciliar commission the same way as a journalist, nor the official observer the same way as the man in the street.[46]

Mgr MacMahon told Osmond Dowling he believed there was 'a serious vacuum in Irish reporting on the Council'. He suggested that theological experts prepare reports and analyses, which could be 'vetted by the bishops and released through something like your office. Meantime certain points of view which assume that every situation can be explained by a progressive reactionary antithesis, hold the field.'[47]

McQuaid commented to Dowling on the coverage of Pope Paul's encyclical, *Mysterium Fidei*:

His [McRedmond's] report on *Mysterium Fidei* was tolerable, John Horgan's lamentable in its ignorance and immaturity. Horgan has met the lightweights. The encyclical has given great satisfaction, as a firm statement of the unchanged and unchanging doctrine of the church ... I hope, as the Council proceeds, the facile division into conservatives and progressives will be cast aside as an outdated cloak for want of knowledge or reflection.[48]

Dowling, in reply, told Mgr MacMahon his impression was that 'Horgan is leading the way and Kevin O'Kelly, Mac Réamoinn and – to a lesser extent – McRedmond may be trying to out-Horgan Horgan. I really blame myself that I did not suggest going out with you for the first few weeks ...'[49]

Mgr MacMahon believes now that the journalists 'did quite a useful job within the limits' and that they 'somehow managed to get what was actually said in the Council by the various speakers'. He says they managed to give 'a much more concrete account, a fuller account, perhaps from a critical point of view, partisan to some extent ...' Canon Battelle says the Council was 'well covered [by the media] but an awful lot of it went over their heads ... over the heads of the ordinary people, and over the heads, even of an awful lot of priests...' Fr Dermod McCarthy believes the 'best purveyor of news about the Council here was radio'. He pays tribute to Seán MacRéamoinn and Kevin O'Kelly, in particular, who 'communicated the possibilities for the church to priests around the country'. Fr Austin Flannery believes the media played a 'huge part' and that people like Horgan and MacRéamoinn 'did so much to bring the message of the Council to the ordinary Irish people'.

Vincent Gallagher praises the journalists, while believing they knew very little on the subjects they were writing about. He welcomes the way they opened up the whole thing. Michael Gill accepts that the journalists were not professional theologians, 'but they had a very intelligent interest in what was going on in the church generally ...' Patrick Masterson thinks the journalists did a 'marvellous job' and lauds them for their commitment and the excitement they generated. Louise Fuller believes popular media coverage 'gave the Council an immediacy and relevance in the general mind, which it would not otherwise have had', and that it also went some way to 'demystifying the mystique which had surrounded the Irish bishops'.[50]

The importance of the Council for Archbishop McQuaid
Archbishop McQuaid faced many issues together, so what priority did he, or could he, give to the Council? Mgr MacMahon believes it was an important issue for him 'at the time and also for the five years or so that were left to him after the Council'. Bishop Murray agrees it was an issue among others, but a major one. Mgr Fehily 'supposes' it was the biggest issue for him at the time. Mgr Stack says it would have to have been number one issue for every bishop because 'they spent four years going and coming from Rome', and in particular for John Charles because he always insisted on doing everything correctly: 'I think it would be very hard for a churchman to avoid realising that the

Council was a watershed.' Mgr Greene, on the other hand, does not think it would have been such a big issue, admitting that his own viewpoint at the time was 'why do we need a Council?'

Archbishop McQuaid's sincere friendship with the Church of Ireland Archbishop of Dublin, George Otto Simms, shows he respected the Council and was keen to spread its message, and he saw it as important in his own life and the life of the church. He gave gifts to Archbishop Simms of each volume of the books on the Council (in French) by Fr Antoine Wenger as they were published. Fr Wenger, editor-in-chief of the French paper, *La Croix*, was a diligent and respected reporter at the Council. He also gave Simms the full set of Council documents.[51]

The Benedictine Abbot of Downside, and later Auxiliary Bishop of Westminster, Dom Christopher Butler, reviewing Wenger's first volume, said it was 'a balanced and thoughtful account by one who is aware of the theological implications of the matters discussed'. He criticised it, however, for being 'if possible, too balanced and "irenic".' He believed Wenger had equal sympathy for the 'progressives' and 'reactionaries' but the pages failed to convey 'to one who was not present at the fateful debates the passion of the drama that was being enacted in them'.[52]

While Archbishop McQuaid concentrated on the Council, he handled his daily correspondence from Rome and dealt promptly with other issues, especially developments in Irish television. Hierarchy minutes for 1963 reveal his close interest in the government proposal to set up comprehensive schools, while the Adoption Bill was another concern.[53] Mgr John O'Regan, Chancellor of the Archdiocese, and the secretaries, were in constant contact with McQuaid during the Council sessions. The reform of the Irish Episcopal Commissions in 1969 showed McQuaid's special interests, as he opted to sit on the commissions for universities, religious, pastoral care/emigrants.[54]

CHAPTER FOUR

Early Attitudes and Initiatives

Fr Chris Mangan, secretary to the archbishop from 1941 to 1957, said John Charles found the Council 'difficult', unlike some bishops who adapted well to it.[1] This is seen from his reaction to another phone call from Bishop Joyce, which Mgr Ardle MacMahon took at the Irish College, 15 November 1962, and noted:

> Bishop Joyce for the Archbishop of Dublin, 8.05 pm.
> Bishop Joyce said the Anti-Curialist group were very active today, especially among the Africans, saying that they have the support of the Pope. Cardinal Gilroy, he said, was worried at this development.

McQuaid's insert: 'This is only one of the alarms to which we shall be subjected all through the Council. And it will get worse.'

> The bishop then asked if Your Grace were speaking tomorrow. I said I did not know of anything that would indicate that Your Grace was, but that Your Grace might or might not be speaking – I did not know.

McQuaid's note at end: 'No. I am not speaking. The issue is not at all clear yet. The Irish bishops have not formulated an unanimous opinion.'[2]

Bishop Joyce, of Irish ancestry, visited the archbishop in Dublin before both the first and second sessions of the Council. He died aged 59, in January 1964, soon after returning from the second session.[3]

McQuaid's pastoral letter, in March 1963, was an early reflection on the Council and indicated that he might be coming to terms with the differences of opinion and accepting the changes to come:

> But as must occur in every Council of the church, each is not at one with all his fellow bishops in at once accepting this or

that way of presenting the truth as fully suited to the needs of the existing world … From the necessary diversity of emphasis and phrasing in the Council will yet result such statement of the unchanging truth, such modification of law and discipline as, for our times and for coming generations, will show forth to men of goodwill, in unsuspected beauty, the glory of the church of Christ.[4]

He showed openness in appointing members of the secret Public Image Committee, December 1963, to 'gather evidence as to the "public image" or "impact" of the church in Dublin and consider means of improving that "image" with a view to strengthening the faith.' He was ready to see where change was needed, but it would be gradual and, at the first meeting it was reported: 'That there is a change, His Grace said, we will all agree, but not a revolution.'[5] His Council correspondence tended to be with conservatives. He commiserated with Mgr Pietro Parente of the Holy Office department of the Roman Curia:

I am grieved by the immoderate utterances in respect of the *Curia Romana*. One might hope that bishops, who are themselves *iudices*, would prove more judicial in the expression of their judgements. But I expect that a certain propaganda has succeeded in clouding the sense of justice in men who are otherwise admirable.[6]

He expressed similar concern to the Public Image Committee, as reported:

The Vatican Council has stimulated criticism which is ignorant. In his book, *Struggle of Minds*, Schillebeeckx [1963] shows himself to be inaccurate and unfair. The man whom His Grace found to be fair, Wenger, has not been made available in English.[7]

Interviews indicate mixed views on the archbishop's attitude to the Council. He told Michael Gill, who visited him at the Irish College, that he had 'grave reservations about what was happening in the Council, that it was something that would pass very, very quickly …'; Mgr Tom Stack believes he was 'very cautious and his instinct would have been resistant to a lot of it'; Mgr Stephen Greene thinks his attitude was '… a bit mixed. It wasn't very favourable, we would have thought ...'; Fr Tony Gaughan says McQuaid 'was not keen on the Council at all'. Louis McRedmond has no doubt McQuaid 'wasn't really happy with the whole conciliar exercise', because people were going to be disturbed and that was why he had to assure them. Patrick Masterson believes he 'must have been a bit alarmed' at the scale of what was going on in the church.

A pastoral letter from Bishop William Philbin of Down & Connor, February 1966, indicated a calming down of expectations about the Council and lessening of its significance in the life of the church. He thanked McQuaid for writing to him about it: 'I am greatly encouraged to have your approval in the line I took. I feel one has to put the brake on this persistent effort to set up a new kind of Catholic Church.'[8]

Bishop Philbin's pastoral inclined to warnings and the need to take care. Expressions were typically: 'not to exaggerate the significance of the change'; 'the principle of authority is not superseded'; '"ecumenism" is a new use of old language'; 'something which is called "the spirit of the Council" or "the mind of Pope John" is appealed to as a substitute for the actual detail of its Decrees'; 'The Vatican Council ... has altered relatively little ...'; 'let no one mislead us into thinking that the church has been cut adrift from its moorings by the Vatican Council'.[9]

Conservatives and liberals

Polarisation of views at the Council led journalists to adopt labels of liberal and conservative for those bishops who were for or against the changes proposed. Individual bishops might favour one change and not another, but the labels, in general, stuck. Liberals were also described as progressive or anti-curial, while conservatives were reactionary or curial.

Louis McRedmond sees Archbishop McQuaid as the 'classical conciliar conservative' who 'fitted in very well with the curia mentality ... and I think he was totally sincere about this ...' Fr Seán Fagan believes he was set in the old mould, but might have foreseen the opening up and then a bit of chaos, and that, perhaps sub-consciously, he felt he would lose control. Canon Paddy Battelle does not agree that McQuaid's mind was 'totally closed' to the Council: 'He was too loyal to Rome ... and to the

Pope, for him to close down [on] anything that emanated under the signature of the Pope'.

He did not trust 'liberal' theologians. He did not want them speaking in his diocese, nor people having access to their works. He feared the Catholic faith might be disturbed. Joseph Foyle says: 'He was like a teacher, this is my patch and I decide what my people, my children are told.'

Interviews indicate that Dublin diocesan priests were as liberal, or as conservative, as others but generally kept their heads down during the McQuaid years. It was McQuaid who appointed Fr Fagan, a Marist priest, to the staff of Mater Dei Institute. He held liberal views, and still does, but McQuaid does not seem to have been worried about him. One day he offered Fr Fagan some newspapers from the United States: 'You have to be very careful; strange things go on in America, terrible stuff. All this stuff about confession.' Fr Fagan was familiar with them, but took them, not admitting that he agreed with them and, in fact, had written at least two articles in *Doctrine & Life* about the new ideas on reform of the sacrament of penance (confession).

McQuaid asked to have certain religious order priests removed from his diocese because he disagreed with their views. One source says Fr David Power, an Oblate, was removed because McQuaid did not like his book on the Eucharist and Fr Michael Hurley believes that perhaps this was so. Another source confirms this story and the full background of how the Oblate Provincial Superior bowed instantly to McQuaid's request and sent Fr Power overnight to a non-job in Rome just as he had been preparing to take up a lecturing post at Milltown Park. Fr Hurley says McQuaid wrote to his Rector, Fr Cecil McGarry, in 1968, asking for him to be removed, but Fr McGarry knew McQuaid well and was 'able to deal with him in a friendly way'. Fr Austin Flannery says McQuaid asked his Provincial, Fr Louis Coffey, to remove him and Fr Fergal O'Connor from the diocese. Ironically, Fr Flannery was standing in for Fr Coffey when McQuaid's letter arrived and he formally acknowledged receipt of it. Fr Coffey did not remove either priest, but pleaded that Fr O'Connor had severe arthritis and might not have so long to live. McQuaid relented. He never wrote nor spoke to any of these priests but dealt only with their superiors.

John Cooney says the Redemptorist Provincial, Fr Jack Whyte, moved Fr Michael O'Connor, editor of *Reality*, to the West Indies, with only ten days notice to leave the country.[10] This was allegedly because McQuaid disliked some articles published in *Reality*, especially a survey of UCD students which 'exploded the myth' that those who went to UCD were 'confirmed in their faith and those who went to Trinity [College] lost it'.[11]

McQuaid's concern at lay people being influenced by new theological views was illustrated when Louis McRedmond met him in Rome during the Council. He was 'very gracious' and then said to him: 'Now, Mr McRedmond, have you read Novak?' Michael Novak was a lay commentator, then progressive in his views, who had recently written a challenging book, *The Open Church*.[12]

> 'Yes, indeed, Your Grace, I have read Novak', and he said to me, 'What do you think of him?' So, I expanded a little, I thought he was very good, I said [about] his approach and his historical understanding and that, and then when I stopped, he said, 'Yes, a pernicious book, Mr McRedmond, a pernicious book'.

Mgr Patrick J. Hamell, editor of *The Irish Ecclesiastical Record*, published a critique of Novak's book by Patrick Masterson and thanked the archbishop for securing

> this splendid and most important article. Dr Masterson's assessment of Novak must be the most searching that has appeared ... It will undo much of the harm caused by the book itself and the uncritical reviews of it that have been published.

McQuaid noted on the letter: 're Novak. You will not read a more accurate and acute analysis.' Early notes for a draft of Dr Masterson's article, but very different from the published version[13] are included with Mgr Hamell's letter[14] and there are editing marks which Masterson confirms were made by his Dean of Faculty of Philosophy & Sociology, at UCD, Mgr John D. Horgan, who had suggested, without indicating McQuaid's involvement, that he write the article.

McQuaid did not like *A New Catechism – Catholic Faith for*

Adults, commonly referred to as the 'Dutch Catechism', prepared by the Dutch Bishops and published soon after the Council.[15] It seemed to confirm his fears about 'liberal' theologians. The Papal Nuncio, Mgr Joseph McGeough, told him in 1968 that Rome had not yet authorised the English translation of the catechism. McQuaid's reply: '… I have never tolerated it, nor shall I, until the Holy See has declared it free from error'.[16]

Early attitudes of Dublin priests and people to the Council

Canon Battelle says the archbishop was surrounded by a group of men 'an awful lot more conservative' than himself, who 'would have moved very slowly where change was concerned'. As regards priests' personal expectations and attitudes to change, Canon Battelle concedes that 'a lot of us who had been ordained in the forties and the fifties were just a little bit slow to let go of the Latin'. Bishop Donal Murray suggests some older priests were difficult.

Mgr Tom Stack sees the Council as 'an extraordinarily important event which I still rejoice in … and a unique experience of opening up and of excitement and of interest in theology'. He says there were priests who looked at 'all this "nonsense" of the Council, saying "we'll get over that too", and the other extreme would be fellows who were "heady" about it and ridiculously romantic, all was going to change'.

Mgr Conor Ward remembers it as 'a marvellous occasion and filtering through, I suppose, already, in the early couple of years of the 60s'. It was 'extremely significant' and fulfilled his expectations. He suggests that the surprise was 'so many participating bishops who wanted to put forward that there must be major change'.

Mgr Jerome Curtin, a Clonliffe College lecturer at the time, says staff did not know a great deal about the Council apart from what they read in the papers and magazines, especially *The Furrow*, and Archbishop McQuaid never addressed them about it. He was surprised no member of the Clonliffe staff was sent out to Rome for the Council so that they could experience the process.

For Cardinal Connell:

It was undoubtedly a time of turmoil and some of us were, I suppose, sufficiently convinced of the value of the order that we had grown up in, to be somewhat sceptical about what was happening and, I suppose, in that sense, I would have been regarded as conservative.

Fr Tony Gaughan admits he was more interested in what he was doing at parish level than in the Council 'as such'. He believes 'quite a lot of other priests' held the same view. One retired priest says it 'upset a lot of the younger priests' when other dioceses seemed to be adopting liturgical changes 'far ahead' of Dublin.

Joseph Foyle says many Dublin priests were for change and brought pressure on Archbishop McQuaid to move quicker with the changes, but they played safe 'on the ground'. Joe Fitz-Patrick feels priests were neither prepared nor educated to implement the changes of Vatican II: 'It was a culture shock really.' Derek Scott believes 'Elderly men would have thought very badly ... of converting to say Mass in English and facing the people and having to sort of have a rapport with them.'

Few of the interviewees mentioned clerical celibacy, but Michael Gill experienced Archbishop McQuaid's concern about the matter. Gill was one of many, priests and laity, who signed a petition in Rome asking the Council Fathers to consider the issue. The *Sunday Independent* later heard about the petition and that the names of Gill and Seán MacRéamoinn were on it. They asked Gill for an article on the subject and he refused, but they ran a story: 'Dublin publisher favours married clergy.' Gill then heard that 'His Grace is deeply disturbed about this', so he wrote to McQuaid, saying the *Sunday Independent* story was not true and he was one of several thousand people who signed the petition, and that if McQuaid had taken offence, he regretted it. McQuaid replied that 'he recalled my meeting [in Rome] and that I was clearly, seriously in need of further theological [education], that this was gravely offensive ... that I was seriously misguided, that I had fallen into the wrong hands ...'. Seán Mac Réamoinn says celibacy was only marginal during the Council: '... the possibilities of a non-celibate ministry would have been mentioned occasionally, but as one of those things a few years down ...'

Vincent Gallagher was impressed by the Council but says people didn't realise how quickly things would change. He believes the 'elimination of Latin from the Mass was a good thing, you can now understand the prayers ...' Michael Gill got the sense that 'there was a lot of enthusiasm'. Elizabeth Lovatt-Dolan welcomed the new emphasis on the church as the People of God and the changes in the liturgy. Derek Scott was very glad that the changes occurred in his time because 'I think they are for the better.' Seán MacRéamoinn found 'a very strong feeling of excitement, relief, or whatever, that there was real movement within the whole church'. Gay Byrne didn't like the English Mass and he still doesn't like it: 'When you lose the mystery and the awe, people get careless.'

The Public Image Committee report in 1964 assessed lay attitudes:

> It would seem that prior to the Council most Irish lay people took it for granted that there was an official line on most, if not all problems, and that bishops more or less all held the same views without having to arrive at them by discussion. The Vatican Council, as reported by the press, presented a very different picture. The laity may now have tended, understandably perhaps, to go to the extreme. The influence of the Vatican Council among the educated and influential classes in Ireland appears to have been very great. Their knowledge of the Council is derived to a great extent from popular reporting. From that reporting the Irish hierarchy appears conservative.[17]

Michael Gill saw a growing interest in theology, but absence of facilities in Ireland for lay people to study it. 'Theology was news, theology mattered,' he says, and through his family publishing company, he contributed to its popularity. The number of books they sold in their Logos series was 'quite extraordinary ... you would not see those numbers now ... it probably began to fall off in the early 70s ...' Patrick Masterson wrote about this phenomenon of 'paperback theology' and how 'suddenly theological issues became fashionable and interesting'. Elizabeth Lovatt-Dolan recalls *Furrow* weekends where priests and lay people got together to discuss theology.

Mater Dei Institute, founded by Archbishop McQuaid, and opened in 1966 within the grounds of Clonliffe College, soon attracted lay people. When Bishop Donal Murray came as a lecturer in 1969, there was a significant number of them and within three or four years 'it was nearly all lay people'. Mgr Stephen Greene says 'One of the great aftermaths of the Council is that the laity have been pursuing ecclesiastical studies and they have been brought into a certain part of the collaborative ministry, but perhaps they feel that they should be in it a little more.'

Public Image Committee
On 31 December 1963, weeks after his return from the second session of the Council, Archbishop McQuaid set up the all-priest, secret, Public Image Committee which has been quoted frequently in this book. Its function was to 'examine what is now called the public image of the church in the Dublin Diocese'. The members were: Mgr Michael O'Halloran, VG (Chairman); Fathers James Kavanagh, Michael O'Neill (Columban), J. Ardle MacMahon, Leo Quinlan, Con Lee, Owen Sweeney, Conor Ward, Joseph Dunn, Roland Burke Savage (Jesuit) and Liam Carey. They would 'gather evidence as to the "public image" or "impact" of the church in Dublin and consider means of improving that "image" with a view to strengthening the faith'. Apart from the report which was issued in June 1964, and an earlier draft report, the diocesan archives contain an account of the first meeting at Archbishop's House, 24 January 1964, when the Archbishop engaged in open, but confidential, discussion on such topics as increased criticism of the church, the impact of the Council, reform of the liturgy and changing attitudes to authority.

Mgr Ward does not remember very much about the Committee but that it was a surprise and the members, apart from the Chairman, were all young priests and could not be seen as 'yes-men'. Mgr Owen Sweeney has a clear recollection and agrees that the Committee was a surprise and the openness of its discussions and recommendations was encouraging. He was soon afterwards re-appointed to work with the emigrant chaplaincy in England but his perception at the time was that the archbishop took very little notice of the Committee's recommendations.

Mgr MacMahon took notes of that first meeting and the copy in the archives has the archbishop's handwritten insertions, implying he approved the overall account. The minutes, with numbers instead of names attributed, are also in the files. The archbishop demanded that the existence and the workings of the committee remain a secret: 'Keep completely to yourselves that you meet, where you meet, who was there – otherwise you will be burdened in your deliberation.' He suggested six months for the report which 'would be lodged in the secret archives where it would be of value in the future ... That there is a change, His Grace said, we will all agree, but not a revolution.' He reiterated the need for secrecy when Fr Joe Dunn said he had heard of the meeting from 'persons outside the group', just two days after being called to it:

> The Archbishop: The importance of secrecy was that it would hinder the deliberations to be pressurised from all sides. Secrecy is essential for good work. Had they noticed that no lay people were on the Committee? This was also so that their deliberations should not be hindered.

Mgr MacMahon noted that the archbishop was 'somewhat disappointed' after that first meeting: '... He felt the discussion centred too much on him personally. The image of the church was not the same as the image of the archbishop'.[20]

The Public Image Committee met 18 times between January and May 1964 and presented its 22-page report to the archbishop on 5 June, dealing with general considerations and then a 'summary of some unfavourable elements in the current image of the church in Dublin, and some suggestions'. The elements were taken under the headings of priests and people, religious, the hierarchy, education, the social apostolate and the communication of ideas. An 'RBS' (Roland Burke Savage) initialled copy of the 'draft' report has comment on the archbishop which was not included in the final report:

> The priests and faithful of the archdiocese feel that like the rest of the Irish bishops, His Grace does not give them that positive leadership which would give them pride and confidence in their church. (The fact that others, delegated by His

Grace, do give a lead does not alter the disillusionment, e.g. had His Grace appeared personally on television to make the laudable appeal in the recent housing crisis, a great impact would have been made on public opinion).[21]

Dublin Diocesan Press Office

In March 1965, Archbishop McQuaid established the Dublin Diocesan Press Office (DDPO) with Osmond G. ('Ossie') Dowling, a *Sunday Independent* journalist, as Director. McQuaid was the first Irish bishop, indeed some believe the first bishop in the world, to make such an appointment, and as early as 1957 he told Bishop Vincent Hanly of Elphin that he had 'a long discussion with Father Connolly on the project of a Press office' and that he would be meeting the editors of the chief newspapers and the Provincial Press Association.[22]

Mgr MacMahon, prompted possibly by the archbishop, noted before the first meeting of the Public Image Committee in 1964: 'How far is the demand for information on church affairs a genuinely responsible one, and how far impertinent? What is the attitude of press, radio and TV in Dublin?' At the first meeting of the Committee: '[Mgr] O'Halloran [chairman] indicated the difficulty of the press in getting diocesan information from the Secretary's desk at Archbishop's House. Would the archbishop not appoint a PRO?'[23]

McQuaid has been rightly praised for the Press Office initiative. Joe Power says it 'surprised everybody', and that McQuaid was 'innovative'. Seán MacRéamoinn was happy in his professional dealings with Dowling and says he certainly did not become 'clericalised'. Joe Fitz-Patrick found Dowling 'very open and supportive' and saw it as a 'progressive move in terms of communication'. Mgr MacMahon, Dowling's day-to-day liaison with the archbishop, believes the Press Office was 'very useful'. He says he had 'many times spoken' to McQuaid about the need for a press office.

The final decision followed rapidly from a suggestion by Dowling who, in a letter to *The Irish Times*, had defended McQuaid against an unproven rumour that his opposition had caused a charity poetry reading in Dublin by actors, Richard

Burton and Elizabeth Taylor, to be cancelled.[24] McQuaid thanked him. Dowling told Mgr MacMahon he seldom wrote letters to the papers, 'but occasionally the weight of nonsense from our fringe of free thinkers and self-styled liberals grows too much to bear ...'[25] Mgr MacMahon invited Dowling to discuss public relations in the diocese and reported to McQuaid that 'the appointment of a full time press officer would be the only effective solution in bringing about a significant improvement.'[26] Mgr MacMahon told McQuaid that Dowling had now offered to 'volunteer his services as a part-time voluntary information officer, should Your Grace prefer not to appoint a full-time press officer at this stage'. A press release on 15 March announced the Office and Dowling's appointment and how it was in accordance with the Council Decree on *The Instruments of Social Communication* and how the media 'today can have such far-reaching effects, for good or for evil, on so many people'.[27]

The archives contain *The Irish Times* editorial, *Experto Credite*, which commented that the news that the 'essentially conservative' Archbishop of Dublin

has appointed a press officer is of considerable interest. To some it may seem surprising that the archbishop feels the need of any such officer. It has been rumoured for some time that the archbishop has been concerned about his public image. Whether that rumour (which is very widespread) has any connection with this appointment it is impossible to say. And if it has, whether such an officer can make any alteration in an image built up over several years remains to be seen ...[28]

Mgr Cecil Barrett commented immediately to McQuaid:

Isn't *The Irish Times* very bitter. They certainly don't like Your Grace's Press Relations Office. But this is not surprising, but rather a healthy sign. This attitude illustrates all the more the need for this new office. Today's leader, though personal and bitter, was poor.[29]

McQuaid stated on 22 April, the day before the Press Office was formally opened with a reception, mainly for journalists, that the purpose was '... to provide a service of news concerning diocesan happenings ... True that press, radio, TV, have given a wide coverage to church events in this diocese. However, the setting up of a service that is professional will improve quantity and quality of information.' John Horgan reported the opening as a 'pleasant, informal affair' and that Archbishop McQuaid 'circulated cheerfully among reporters after the speeches, saying that he was sure that they would be glad of the opportunity to "see the ogre in his den".'[30]

Mgr MacMahon wrote to Dowling from Rome, September 1965, saying the Press Office had secured a greater 'presence' of the diocese, and of the church, in the Irish media of communication and in *The Catholic Herald*, and that the purpose of such a presence was 'pastoral, to secure the minds and hearts of the people of God' by communicating the message of the gospel. Dowling was to visit Rome for the conclusion of the Council but he got a virus infection.[31]

In October, Dowling spoke to a Pax Romana meeting in Carlow on 'The Layman and Communication within the Church'. The script indicates certain inputs from Mgr MacMahon and Archbishop McQuaid. Dowling reported to McQuaid: 'I do not think my paper was a particularly popular one with Pax Romana, though they were kind enough to compliment me on it.' He told Mgr MacMahon that, as expected, he was in 'quite a hot seat' and this was evident from the discussion and questions after his paper:

> It really does still continue to astonish me the widespread and deep-seated animosity towards us – I mean, the diocese, in certain quarters. Because these people are more ready – and more able – to talk, one could very easily, of course, over estimate their influence.[32]

Louis McRedmond wrote in 1966 that the press office was 'still to be seen as a place where frank questions will be frankly answered'. Mgr MacMahon noted to McQuaid in 1967 that Douglas Gageby, editor of *The Irish Times*, had been asked on television how the appointment of Dowling had helped him and replied that Dowling 'did "funnel" some news in the way of his newspaper'. McQuaid underlined *some news* and noted: 'A gentleman would have been generous.'[33]

Dowling, a friendly, well-liked man, seems generally to have had a good working relationship with the archbishop and Mgr MacMahon but there were tensions and instances of McQuaid's exactness which could have annoyed others. Dowling's letters to him always had to be handwritten, following the etiquette laid down by him, and they always started 'My Lord Archbishop' and concluded 'Your Grace's obedient servant'. On one occasion, in the cold of January, Dowling apologised for typing: 'My hands are cold and if I were to write it you would not be able to read it.'[34]

Dowling had direct access to the archbishop, although Mgr MacMahon could be described as his 'line manager'. Dowling was quite informal in expressing his views, without fear or excessive awe, the sort of positive approach seen also in McQuaid's correspondence with Fr Joe Dunn and Fr Burke Savage.[35] But, there were tensions in the relationship, with Dowling not always given sufficient information, as he noted to Mgr MacMahon on several occasions, such as before the Mansion House meeting in January 1966 (see chapter 6):

> If I am invited to the function in the Mansion House on Tuesday next, I will be happy to accept, without necessarily becoming involved in or interfering with the press relations on that occasion. If, however, I am personally or through you instructed by His Grace, or requested by Father Burke Savage to assist in dealing with the press on Tuesday night, I will certainly do so provided that I am given in advance all the information that I require ...[36]

McQuaid was annoyed when Dowling pressed him for a photocall at Archbishop's House in Drumcondra for the visit of Archbishop Ramsey of Canterbury with Archbishop Simms, in 1967. He had earlier declined but Dowling persisted. He then replied: 'Photographers will not be welcome at my house, but I shall tolerate their presence for Fr Arrupe [a separate visit by the Jesuit General] and Archbishop Ramsey ... You will not take my reconsideration as evidence that, because I am pressed, I shall yield in other cases.'[37]

In 1968, journalist T. P. O'Mahony reported the introduction of a two-tier minimum income scheme for Dublin parish priests and curates.[38] He had approached Dowling who was unaware of it, as he had not been informed. Dowling inquired and was told it was only being considered, then that it was purely an administrative matter and of no concern to the press.[39] McQuaid was the first bishop in the country to introduce such a scheme, another practical demonstration of his care for his priests. It reflected the Public Image Committee's recommendation for an adequate pension scheme for clergy and measures to deal with the disparity in salaries for curates: 'Curacies and parishes tend to be judged, not by the scope they offer for apostolic zeal, but solely by a financial consideration: "How much is it worth?"'[40]

On another occasion, Dowling offered to resign because he released information before an embargo McQuaid had set without informing him.[41] Dowling again complained when Fr Paul Freeney published an article in *Doctrine & Life* on the Post-Ordination Pastoral Course, saying he was not told in advance and was embarrassed when the media asked him about it. McQuaid noted Dowling's 'formal protest'

> but I should have thought that you would have sent me a letter of sympathy because one of my priests, without the slightest reference to me, printed such a report on a confidential meeting. Confidence may be abused, but we must still believe in Confidence and live on that basis.

Fr Freeney had reported on the meeting of 200 priests, an intriguing few days 'but mainly because the priests present were indeed critical, and few diocesan sacred cows escaped unscathed, yet not a harsh word was spoken, there was no call for revolution, and any criticisms made were both serious and charitable'. He had added that 'above all there was no rancour, no harsh criticism, no angry young men. Bishop Carroll expressed pride at the tone of the meeting.'[43]

It would seem that, despite these hiccups, McQuaid appreciated the work Dowling did for him and he showed his gratitude. His comment to Papal Nuncio, Mgr Gaetano Alibrandi, in 1970 reflected a changing attitude to communications: 'Five years experience of the Dublin Diocesan Press Office has shown the value of having a journalist as Director ... Could communications form part of the civics syllabus?'.[44] Dowling tried to change him further with a five-page memo:

I do not subscribe to the opinion that there is in the press a great deal of hostility towards us. What is true, however, is the fact that there is a great awareness in press circles of our tendency to regard communications as a one-way street. This is not conducive to the best relations. It is not, indeed, remarkable to find newspapers viewing with a cold eye statements emanating from a source noted for its reluctance to offer comment when requested. Nobody appreciates better than I that some areas are delicate. On the other hand, many refusals have seemed either unnecessary or unwise ... Our Lord was never afraid to answer questions or to engage in disputation. Even in the market place.[45]

World Communications Day

The archbishop invited journalists and editors to a Mass and reception in Clonliffe College to celebrate World Communications Day, May 1967. Dowling had suggested that since 'some Protestants will be on the invitation list, and it will be made clear that they may come only for the reception, would it also be considered an ecumenical thought to invite the Church of Ireland press officer [Rev R.A.Warke]'. McQuaid noted: 'He can do no harm.'[46] His sermon at the Mass referred to journalists' lives being:

passed in a whirlwind of events that are swept together in the disarray of human passion. Not yours the hermit-like seclusion in which the tranquil scholar can collect, assess and finally judge the evidence. You are obliged to be concerned with the concrete, the tangible, the vividly present, especially the fleeting and sensational. An avid public will not allow you the time that you yourselves would wish to have for due reflection.[47]

The Irish Times praised the sermon for being marked 'not only by understanding of problems but also by compassion and clear-sightedness...'[48] John Horgan saw it as a sign that McQuaid was changing and wished to have better relations with the press and thanked him '... for your kindness in meeting and entertaining us' and 'for the sympathy and understanding in your sermon'.[49]

Mater Dei Institute

Archbishop McQuaid was praised for establishing Mater Dei Institute. Fr Eltin Griffin: 'great credit is due to him ...'; Cardinal Connell: '... very much ahead of his time in making that decision, which he did in conjunction with Mother Jordana, the Dominican nun'; Patrick Masterson: '... forward-thinking'; and a parish priest who was then on the staff of Clonliffe College says '... from the word go it was a success, but he wouldn't, he didn't, he consulted nobody'. Judging it to be 'one of the greatest' of McQuaid's contributions, Mgr MacMahon says it would not have been a result of the Council, but 'would have been in line with insights he already had'. Agreeing it was 'farsighted', Mgr Conor Ward also says Mater Dei would have come from McQuaid's own stated policies and his interest in education, and he was probably thinking of the need to have people, 'qualified in a safe location like his own'. This reference to a 'safe location' ties in with the concern McQuaid is believed to have had for the orthodoxy of teaching at Maynooth in the 1960s.[50] His response was to withdraw his students from Maynooth and strengthen Clonliffe, linking it, and then Mater Dei, with the Angelicum University in Rome for degrees in theology.

Mater Dei was not initially intended for the laity although it soon become predominantly so. It opened in 1966 with 35 nuns beginning a three year course in theology.[51] Mgr Joseph Carroll, President, Clonliffe College, said Mater Dei had been founded

> to give Religious Sisters and members of secular institutes the theological training which will be of benefit to them in their own personal lives and to the task committed to them by the archbishop of imparting religious instruction to the youth of the diocese.[52]

Telefís Éireann (TÉ)

Irish television started on New Year's Eve, 1961. The Hierarchy Television Committee, in October 1959, had called for the bishops to see that the church, 'as custodian of faith and morals, has the machinery to make her influence felt on the new medium from the very beginning'.[53]

Archbishop McQuaid tried unsuccessfully to gain control

over television coverage of religious matters. Cathal Canon McCarthy, President, Clonliffe College, was his unofficial liaison in Radio Éireann. Canon McCarthy favoured 'informality' and never giving his office any particular title, 'a policy which, I think, has resulted in smoothness'. McQuaid agreed: 'Your value to me lies in your present anonymity and your established good relations with Mr L. O Broin [Secretary of the Department of Posts & Telegraphs]'.[54] However, McQuaid saw need for the arrangement to become more formally recognised as his concern for some control over the new television station grew. He wrote to Eamonn Andrews, Chairman, Radio Éireann:

> I have appointed as my personal liaison priest in Dublin, the city and the diocese in which is situated the Television Centre, the Very Rev Canon Cathal McCarthy, Holy Cross College, Clonliffe. It is my hope that this appointment will facilitate the necessary consultations between the Television Authority and the Archbishop of Dublin. I will be glad to co-operate with the Authority in all that pertains to my office.[55]

Dermot O'Flynn, Supreme Knight of St Columbanus, saw 'urgent need for the selection and training of an elite to recover these vital lines of communication [TÉ] of ideas to the general public'. He gave McQuaid a report in 1962, stating only four of the 16 television producers were Catholics – Jim Fitzgerald, James Plunkett, Gerard Victory and Chloe Gibson and, of these, only the last two were 'practising' Catholics. The others included Shelah Richards, producer of Religious Programmes, who was 'a divorced actress', and Jack White, in charge of all religious programmes, who was 'a non-Catholic and a liberal'. O'Flynn said the report came from a 'reliable source'. A second report, seemingly also from O'Flynn, profiled a number of lay people, not just in broadcasting, but in other areas of public life, with the inference that they were not safe people to have on television.[56]

McQuaid told Canon McCarthy that he gave Archbishop Morris of Cashel & Emly as his 'definite opinion' that he should be the bishops' national director at TÉ.

> ... I cannot see the present arrangements effecting any worthwhile results that would firmly establish in the station

our policy or our prestige ... the good of the faith is what we must consider.[57]

Illness took Canon McCarthy out of contention for the post of priest director, but the hierarchy agreed:

that the Archbishops of Dublin and Cashel should approach the Taoiseach without delay to express the grave concern of the hierarchy concerning the personnel in Telefís Éireann and to protest against the appointment of unbelievers to key posts. It was also agreed that Fr Joseph Dunne [sic], who had training in television, be appointed a whole-time executive assistant for religious broadcasting to Telefís Éireann, and that he act under the direction of the Chairman of [Hierarchy] Television Committee ...[58]

Correspondence continued and the issue changed to crisis while Archbishop McQuaid was at the next session of the Council. Canon McCarthy wrote to him, in November 1963, that Kevin McCourt, Director General, TÉ, had phoned to say that the TÉ authority 'at their meeting yesterday, appointed Fr Dodd OP, as priest director. I must say the news came as a great shock to me: for more reasons than one I felt sure that Fr Joe Dunn would be accepted.' McQuaid replied from Rome to this 'surprising' letter and that he had written directly to McCourt 'thanking him for the courtesy of having communicated his decision to me through you and stating that, though I am the sole authority in this diocese in which his station is situated, I know neither the priest nor his competence'.[59]

Kevin McCourt told McQuaid that the [Hierarchy's] Catholic Television Interim Committee

accepted a condition of the Authority that it should have the selecting of a suitable person, and a short list of four names was submitted to me by the Committee for that purpose – the fourth being subsequently not available, I was told – it seemed to me that Father Romuald Dodd OP, in all respects would be most suitable ... I cannot but feel that your letter implies your disapproval of the nomination made by the Catholic Television Interim Committee ...[60]

McQuaid replied that he did not know a list had been presented, that he was unaware of a priest being appointed, that he received news of an appointment at second hand and 'that I do not know the priest appointed in my diocese, where it is the archbishop who is responsible for religious affairs'.[61] The archbishop's control in TÉ (later RTÉ) effectively ended with Dodd's appointment and he realised it within a month when a controversial, liberal theologian appeared on TÉ.

Mgr MacMahon told McCourt that the archbishop had directed him to write and ask him to state 'by whose authority Rev Gregory Baum OSA, who appeared on a TÉ programme, was invited to speak and did speak in this diocese on matters of faith and morals.' McCourt replied that Fr Baum had been interviewed in connection with the proceedings of the Vatican Council and since he was 'a well-known expert on the ecumenical movement and was attached to the Council', it was taken for granted he was well qualified to comment on the proceedings there. McCourt said TÉ were responsible for using Fr Baum's services 'but we would assume that, if he required ecclesiastical clearance to participate in the programme of the kind involved, this would be a matter between him and the ecclesiastical authorities'. McQuaid's note, 18/12/63: 'No answer sent.'[62] There was not any further correspondence.

McQuaid remained critical of Fr Dodd. Replying to Canon McCarthy, who was worried about the presentation of 'religious and para-religious programmes on TV' and that there seemed to be no one 'who keeps a watch on them', he wrote, in 1968: 'I am glad to have your note, for it confirms what I have always held … When I consider the care with which you treated radio matters, I am shocked by the nonchalance or failure of the present controller, Father Dodd.'[63]

CHAPTER FIVE

Trying to Live the Dream in Dublin

Archbishop McQuaid found the aftermath of the Council difficult, feeling there was more change coming than had ever been
intended by it. He diligently, but cautiously, implemented the
directives he received from Rome, but seemed unwilling to go
further. Some priests and lay people became impatient and there
were frequent media attacks, but he stood his ground with
strong support from many of the older priests. He pioneered
some initiatives in the diocese – Diocesan Press Office, Diocesan
Council of Priests, new commissions, Mater Dei Institute, for
example, but he was most concerned that the 'simple faithful'
would not be confused or disturbed in their traditional faith or
religious practice.

He spoke in the Pro-Cathedral, Dublin, on return from the
final session of the Council, December 1965. The text of his address was issued by the Diocesan Press Office:

> ... You may, in the last four years, have been disturbed at
> times by reports about the Council. May I who have assisted
> at every meeting of the Council assure you that the Council
> was a wondrous example of dignity and seriousness and
> courtesy. You may have been worried by much talk of
> changes to come. Allow me to reassure you. No change will
> worry the tranquillity of your Christian lives. For, time after
> time, Pope John XXIII and our present Holy Father have in-
> sisted – but the point has been sadly missed – that our delib-
> erations in the Council had only one purpose: to search the
> deposit of the faith, to look more deeply into the teaching of
> the church that we, the faithful, the religious and the priests
> and bishops might be able to meet more firmly the changed
> circumstances of our present world ... As the months will
> pass, gradually the Holy Father will instruct us how to put

into effect the enactments of the Council. With complete loyalty, as children of the one, true church, we fully accept each and every decree of the Vatican Council.[1]

'No change' was the headline which emerged from this address. It was misleading and it misled. To this day, as soon as the words 'John Charles McQuaid' and 'Vatican Council' are spoken to people old enough to remember, the almost immediate response is 'No change'.

Joe Fitz-Patrick was 'just gob-smacked'. Fr Dermod McCarthy asked himself if the archbishop were correct, then, 'what was all the fuss about?' He claims priests about ten years older than him were 'apoplectic'. Louis McRedmond says McQuaid said very little at the Council but 'his big statement was the famous one at the end, about not disturbing the tranquillity etc.' Maeve McRedmond says it portrayed 'a patronising attitude. Don't think you will be disturbed, children ...' John Horgan admits 'many people in the media, probably myself included ... leapt on this as an example of how far behind the times he [McQuaid] was'. Desmond Fisher later interpreted it '... that Vatican II would make no change in the peaceful life of the church in Ireland'.[2]

Bishop Donal Murray says one has 'to parse and analyse' anything McQuaid said, and that on this occasion he didn't tell his people there would be no change, but that change wouldn't ruffle the tranquillity of their Christian life. He suggests he was more worried about the tranquillity being ruffled than about the changes themselves. Mgr Tom Fehily says McQuaid had a way of putting things across 'in a very archaic way' and he meant 'there would be no doctrinal change' and the doctrine did not change. Mgr Stephen Greene was with other priests in the Pro-Cathedral and they were 'surprised' because they were under a different understanding due to press reports. Canon Paddy Battelle suggests McQuaid spoke in this way because 'he himself didn't understand the wind of change that was coming. I don't think any prophet or seer would have foreseen that.' Mgr Jerome Curtin, however, saw it as the indication that he would 'totally fulfil every instruction he got from Rome' but agrees that 'emotionally he found it difficult'. Mgr Ardle MacMahon agrees he could have said it in a better way, but meant it to be a reassurance to his people. He sees the approach as '... expressive of the approach of bishops at that time. They were the shepherds and the shepherd had to care for his flock ... But at that precise moment, probably, it wasn't well-timed ...'

Archbishop McQuaid's consistency is seen when the Pro-Cathedral address is read alongside the letter to his priests on the eve of the Council in 1962, to his priests from Rome, 23 November 1965, and in the context of the hierarchy group statement from Rome, 8 December.[3] He told his priests in November 'that we should all thank God for the happy conclusion of a Council that has been so visibly guided by God the Holy Ghost and that, for centuries to come, must influence the church in her thought and discipline ...', and that the Pope asked for prayers that 'we may be able, in the years ahead, to understand more clearly the traditional and authentic teaching of the church, as set forth by the Council ...'[4] The hierarchy stated that during the past four years the Council had been 'prayerfully studying the heritage of divine truth which the church has received from God and the fruit of this meditation is now embodied in a great series of constitutions and decrees ... We now face the great challenge of implementing the decisions of the Council ... In the years to come ... there will be many changes in the external life of the church ...'[5] Archbishop Morris of Cashel & Emly agreed with McQuaid – who he admitted was too conservative for his taste – that 'it was a good time to reassure people'.[6]

The 'No Change' address has been contrasted with Pope Paul's address to the Italian bishops, three days previously. Asked whether everything would remain the same after the Council, the Pope said: 'The spirit of the Council says, NO! I, we, and we above all, must make some change – and it will not be a trifling change'.[7] It is surprising that in the three weeks after McQuaid's address, which so many people still remember so vividly, there was only one letter in *The Irish Times*,[8] and none in the *Irish Independent*.

Implementing the decisions of the Council

Archbishop McQuaid had respect for the Council documents, as in his gratitude when Papal Nuncio Sensi gave him 'as a personal gift from the Holy Father', a copy of each of two books on the Council: *Ss. Oecumenicum Concilium Vaticanum II. Constitutiones, Decreta, Declarationes* and *I Padri Presenti al Concilio Ecumenico Vaticano II.* The second title, in Italian, was the complete presentations made by the Fathers to the Council.[9] His gifts to Archbishop Simms of Fr Wenger's books on the Council and then of the entire set of decrees was a further indication of this respect, as was his donation of the decrees to the Church of Ireland Training College.[10]

Many of the changes, especially in liturgy, were not mentioned in the Council documents. Bishop Murray understands the archbishop's confusion, 'because he was at the Council and he thought he knew what was said, and still the thing was pushing on and on ...' Mgr Patrick Corish believes a lot was done in the name of the Council about which the Council never spoke, but people felt they had to stay on the bandwagon. Referring to the 'spirit of the Council', he says the Council said nothing about removing Latin nor about the priest having to face the people at Mass. Cardinal Connell is not 'too sure' that McQuaid 'would altogether have understood the enthusiasm for change manifested in some of those involved in the Council' nor that he 'would have been in sympathy with the spirit in which changes were coming'. McQuaid warned in a pastoral letter that it was 'not a renewal in the spirit of the Second Vatican Council to change the certain teaching of the church of Christ for the partial vision of a private judgement. One may not tamper with the doctrine of the church'.[11]

Whatever the spirit was, Louis McRedmond was struck by it in Rome: 'When I got home I found a local church that was not imbued with the spirit of the Council', but 'even if the spirit wasn't around [in Dublin] the people wanted to know all about it' and this was shown in the great attendances at the Milltown Park public lectures.

Implementation of Council documents and directives
Giacomo Cardinal Lercaro of Bologna, a leading reformer at the Council, headed the body in Rome for overseeing liturgical reforms. He wrote to Cardinal Conway, January 1966, and to the chairmen of other national bishops' conferences, suggesting

guidelines and asking how the reforms were working in practice.[12] Cardinal Conway was asked to pass this secret letter 'only' to the bishops.

Cardinal Lercaro noted places where the adoption of the vernacular in the Mass had given rise to 'some signs of disquiet' and supported bishops who might decide to retain some Latin Masses in big cities and in places where there were a lot of tourists. He suggested 'prudence should be our guide' about the priest at Mass facing the people. Provisional altars were gradually to disappear and give way to more permanent structures. If the tabernacle were to be in a place other than the altar, the bishop 'must judge whether or not all requirements are met in the alternative proposal'. Cardinal Lercaro left each bishop to decide the best approach to implementation for his own diocese.[13] It is clear that Archbishop McQuaid followed these secret suggestions exactly.

Bishop Murray points to 'considerable evidence' that McQuaid 'tried very hard' in implementing the Council. One retired priest believes he implemented 'reluctantly'. Joe FitzPatrick says 'there was very little encouragement or leadership from "head office" ...'. Maeve McRedmond says that far from implementing the Council, McQuaid gave 'little support' to priests like Michael Hurley and Austin Flannery who tried. John Brophy remembers deadlines for implementing changes being set by the hierarchy and in Dublin, in particular, 'on the due date and not a day before it, nor a day after, these things happened'. Seán MacRéamoinn says in Dublin, in particular, the changes came slowly and 'the laity were certainly not following any great guidance from the leaders of the church locally ...' Fr Tom Butler refers to priests who had been 'hyped up by the media' to expect all sorts of things, and who thought the archbishop 'should have done more, and more rapidly'.

John Horgan asked Mgr MacMahon, February 1966, to tell McQuaid 'how glad and grateful we all are for the extent and nature of the liturgical changes announced over the weekend. For the first time, it seems, the English (or Irish) Mass is to be regarded as the norm, and the Latin as the exception'.[14]

One retired priest remembers how the new diocesan commissions on liturgy, music and so on, were 'packed' with top people in the diocese 'to keep the young crowd quiet', there was no consultation and if any put their heads 'above the parapet' they were 'shot at fairly sharply'. Fr Austin Flannery recalls a Dominican colleague of his, Fr Liam Walsh, who resigned in protest from the liturgy commission because he felt McQuaid was handling it badly and implementation was proceeding too slowly. Fr Walsh was then removed from all other positions he held in the diocese, including Mater Dei Institute.

The procedure was that Rome issued directives and national hierarchies then drew up details of how they would implement them, submitted them back to Rome and waited for approval. Fr Dermod McCarthy recalls delays with implementation being approved because those 'who had been left to implement were the people back in the Curia ... They dragged their feet.'

Sometimes even McQuaid wondered why Rome was delaying, asking Cardinal Conway:

> ... if we could have official approval of the Preface in the vernacular. The people are disconcerted by a fragmentary approval and would greatly welcome a clear cut at the *Te Igitur*. The French had their Preface approved, I see, in January which is late for them.[15]

Conway sent McQuaid the translation of the Canon of the Mass, 20 September 1967, and McQuaid thanked him, saying: 'At first sight, it reads to one who has used the sonorous Latin, a pedestrian composition despite the explanatory appendix.'[16] When Conway told him, in 1970, that changes in the *Missa Chrismata* on Holy Thursday would not be enforced that year, McQuaid noted: 'Ackd: glad no more changes this year. Priests and people have had as much change as they can manage.'[17] He does not say he himself cannot 'manage' change, but it is his priests and people, a way of speaking he frequently used, without consultation. He was often critical of how Rome communicated its decisions and suggested to Conway '... that the Holy See [Rome] consider how it could make known its decrees or pronouncements to residential bishops, if not before, at least as soon as, the organs of the secular press are given a release'.[18]

There are still mixed views on how the changes should have been implemented. Mgr MacMahon thinks 'the pace was probably right'. Religious journalist, Joe Power believes it was too rapid, even in Dublin, and a lot of people were upset by it. He says documents were interpreted by theologians who had a 'liberal frame of mind' leading, for instance, to the summary removal of statues and side altars in churches and the end of devotions like the Miraculous Medal and the Confraternity which had been very popular with the laity before the Council. Mgr MacMahon told Osmond Dowling in May 1965 that the Press Office would respond to the claim that the archbishop was slower than other bishops in implementation of conciliar directives, by saying that more adjustments were required in a diocese with over 100 parishes and three-quarters of a million Catholics than in smaller dioceses.[19] Fr Burke Savage defended McQuaid:

> ... Other bishops have moved faster. Very good, but does that necessarily prove that they have been wiser? ... the archbishop's point of view is at the very least arguable: don't interfere too suddenly with the established patterns of things; novelty for novelty's sake is a nine days wonder; habits that are slowly formed are most lasting.[20]

When G. J. Bergin of Clondalkin asked Osmond Dowling about the varying pace of implementation of the liturgical changes, from diocese to diocese, he replied that it had been left to the bishops of each country to decide what prayers in the vernacular would be introduced first, 'and each bishop was responsible for implementing this decision in his diocese ... So far, in the Dublin diocese, the first steps have been taken. Other changes will follow, but the process will be gradual.'[21]

As late as 1971, Dowling told Mgr MacMahon that a parishioner from Clogher Road claimed widespread dissatisfaction there because 'over a year after the new liturgy was supposed to be implemented, there is still no effort being made in St Bernadette's to introduce such things as the Offertory Procession'. Dowling agreed that Clogher Road, contrary to his informant's belief, might not be the only one out of step at all, 'because I know of another parish where lay readers have not yet made an appearance at Sunday Mass'.[22]

It is clear that obedience led Archbishop McQuaid in implementing the Council changes, whether or not he agreed personally. He gave absolute obedience to Rome and, in turn, expected it also from his priests and people. Mgr Fehily says he 'was interested in obeying everything ...'; Vincent Gallagher: 'he was so diligent a disciple that he accepted it completely'; Mgr MacMahon: '... his approach was always obedience to the Holy See, obedience to authority' and he carried out the requirements of the Council 'exactly'; Louis McRedmond: '...he was obedient in doing what, I presume, Rome required him to do, but it would be hard to detect any great enthusiasm for conciliar attitudes'. One retired priest believes 'most men in those days who were good at ruling were also good at obeying'.

Concelebration

Archbishop McQuaid had difficulty with the introduction of concelebration, several priests together saying the same Mass, as already referred to in the Council debate on the liturgy. It arose at consecrations, or 'ordinations', of new bishops in the later years, and he did his best to avoid it. Archbishop Joseph Cunnane of Tuam invited him, in 1969, to his episcopal ordination:

> I wish to invite you, if you wish, to join with some of the other bishops in concelebrating the Mass. I realise, however, that you may not wish to do this, and I leave the matter entirely in Your Grace's own hands.

McQuaid's note: 'Please excuse.' He accepted the invitation to the ordination 'but not to lunch'.

Some months earlier, when Mgr Joseph Carroll, President of Clonliffe College, was appointed auxiliary Bishop of Dublin, there was no reference to concelebration and the ceremony was very clearly described as 'consecration' in the pre-conciliar style. Mgr Carroll told the archbishop in a telegram from Rome before the consecration: 'New Rite of Consecration not obligatory. Old Rite may be used.'[24] Inviting McQuaid to Monaghan for his ordination as bishop in January 1970, Bishop Patrick Mulligan of Clogher wrote: 'If you can come, perhaps you would like me to arrange accomodation [sic] and if you wish to concelebrate.' McQuaid's note; 'Yes: I hope to be present, but as I shall drive up that morning, may I be excused from concelebrating.'[25]

McQuaid did not always refuse concelebration for others, as when Fr Liam Carey requested it for nine diocesan priests participating in a residential Youth Leadership Seminar. McQuaid's note: 'Yes, if rubrics strictly observed.'[26] From January 1971, he allowed marriages in Dublin up to 4.30 pm and concelebration of Mass was now permitted at both marriages and funerals.[27]

In 1970, he was warning against liturgical celebration and liturgical prayer replacing personal and private prayer, fearing the fundamentals of Christian faith might be softened. Archbishop Finbar Ryan, then retired from Trinidad, and back living in Cork, was of the same mind: 'The great need, as I see it, is to inspire our people – priests, religious and laity – with realisation of the need for personal prayer.' Commenting on a letter from McQuaid, he wrote: 'I share your distress about the rosary, especially about its rejection by priests and religious.'[28]

Caution characterised Archbishop McQuaid's approach to the conciliar changes. Vincent Gallagher, Mgr MacMahon and Fr Tom Butler, all of whom knew him well, approved of this. Fr Butler believes he wanted change, but 'gently', and he didn't want the people to be upset: 'It was the people of his diocese that he had at heart. I think he knew that the priests would be OK ...' He believes he wanted the Council, and its values, to be put into practice, but 'slowly, slowly' because 'he was afraid, I think, of the reaction of the Irish people ...' Mgr MacMahon agrees he moved at a 'somewhat slower pace than some countries moved' but, as a result, he had fewer negative and traditionalist reactions.

Canon Battelle says that, when a change came, McQuaid wanted to consider its possible faults and excesses before allowing it. He does not believe he expected it all to 'blow over' and for things to be back to what they were, but he doesn't think a 'great deal of change took place in McQuaid's mind'. Fr Tony Gaughan, believes he was 'cautious' and that

> it was probably difficult for him more than anybody else, being at the top, in the sense that the buck stops at the top, and it is very difficult when you haven't unanimity about change. So, it was difficult to drive a middle course.

Vincent Gallagher believes McQuaid was anxious to be seen

'as a person who wished to go along with Vatican II, but doing it slowly' and that this best suited Irish traditions. Maeve McRedmond believes 'he wanted things to go on as they were'. Joe Power holds that he didn't want to see too much change but 'always gave the impression that changes which were on the way were good'. In his draft reply to Tim Pat Coogan (1965), McQuaid said 'undoubtedly the process of *aggiornamento* is affecting the church in every country. And it is worth remembering that this involves new emphasis on old truths, rather than new truths.'[29]

Control of change
Canon Battelle believes McQuaid was not against change 'but he would like to control change himself ...' Fr Seán Fagan says he 'wasn't interested in any kind of change that he couldn't control ... But for people quoting Vatican II or saying "the Vatican wants this or that", he would have to check the canon law to see what status it had'. McQuaid didn't like experimentation unless he knew what was going on and Fr Butler remembers him saying: 'They are not going to experiment in my diocese.' He believes McQuaid would have been easier on paraliturgy, celebrations not directly affecting the Mass or the sacraments, but when it came to basics like the Mass, 'his whole theological background, his age, his devotion to the Eucharist, naturally, wouldn't allow it'.

Communications Centre/Catholic Communications Institute of Ireland
In June 1964, the hierarchy appointed Fr Joe Dunn 'Director of a Communications Centre, at an honorarium of 200 pounds a year to be paid out of the Hierarchy General Fund'. Archbishop Morris of Cashel & Emly said it would serve 'as a meeting place for those engaged in Catholic television work and would be helpful in the recruiting and training of new talent'.[30] The site, building and equipment for the £55,000 Centre at Booterstown, Co Dublin, which opened in February 1967, were provided from the funds of the Catholic Truth Society of Ireland. Annual running costs were budgeted for between £9,000 and £10,000 a year with a grant of 12,000 dollars from the Holy See for the first year. Charges for the communications courses and voluntary contri-

butions would make up the deficit. The Radharc television unit was one of the activities based at the Centre.[31]

The archbishop, Mgr MacMahon and Osmond Dowling were soon isolated from the Communications Centre and ignored with regard to its activities. Dowling commented to McQuaid who said, 'There will be plenty more of the same.'[32] A serious instance of 'more of the same' was when Bishop Herlihy of Ferns launched the *Irish Ecumenism Directory* at a press conference in Dublin and Dowling knew nothing until the *Evening Herald* rang him afterwards. Dowling told McQuaid, who noted: 'I was unaware either that the Directory was to be published or that Ferns would give a press conference in my See City.' Dowling asked Fr Kevin McNamara, who had arranged the press conference, for a copy of the Directory but Fr McNamara said he hadn't a spare copy, 'However, it is being published by CTSI and is expected within ten days.' Mgr MacMahon expressed displeasure to Fr McNamara and that 'apart from other considerations, the matter proved a distinct embarrassment to His Grace owing to the resentment expressed by the press to His Grace's Diocesan Press Office.'[33]

Archbishop McQuaid was not consulted when the Catholic Communications Institute of Ireland (formed in October 1969 by the merger of the Communications Centre, the Catholic Truth Society of Ireland – re-named Veritas – and the Communications Council) advertised for a 'Writer-Publicist'. Mgr MacMahon expressed fear that closure of the Diocesan Press Office would 'no longer be an option but a necessity', probably within a year. McQuaid did not accept this. He had discussions with Fr Joe Dunn, Director of the Institute, who told him that the 'Writer-Publicist' would only work in the Catholic Truth Society office. I got the job and it was finally titled 'Assistant Editor, Veritas Publications'. I was unaware of the sensitivity it had caused and never had any communication with Archbishop McQuaid, Mgr MacMahon or Osmond Dowling about it.[34]

Collegiality
Collegiality, the bishops of a country or region, acting as a college, with the Pope, and each retaining autonomy in his own diocese, was an important outcome of the Council, but did not

feature strongly in these interviews. The role of national bishops' conferences was developed after the Council. It is common practice, now, for bishops' conferences to adopt policies, issue statements and act as a college. The Irish bishops' conference was, in the eighteenth century, one of the first to be established. It is a loose structure without any permanent secretariat but had sub-committees, even before the Council. Bishop Willie Walsh of Killaloe says that, even now, the conference can make a decision and 'I can say, sorry, we're not implementing that in Killaloe and the conference has no legal power to do so ... each one is ultimately responsible to Rome'.[35]

The government was interested in the collegiality debate at the Council and its implications for the bishops as a lobby group in the social and educational fields. Tommy Commins, Irish Ambassador to the Holy See, told Hugh McCann, Secretary, Department of External Affairs in Dublin, in 1963, that while the implications for the secular government were obvious,

> what our bishops think collectively on the subject I am not in a position to say but, certainly, Archbishop McQuaid as well as Dr Browne of Galway have expressed themselves ... as opposed to the grant of power to the National Episcopal Conference which could or might be held to limit or modify in any way the supreme power exercised by an individual bishop in his own diocese.[36]

One priest, who was close to McQuaid, believes the Council's approach to collegiality created a very big change overnight, almost pointing to a democratic style of government. He says this was new to McQuaid and he did not find it easy, being concerned that collegiality might undermine both the primacy of the Pope and the bishop in his own diocese. He congratulated Mgr Pietro Parente of the Holy Office who had spoken at the Council, November 1963:

> It seems to me, if I am correct, that there is much confused thinking about *collegialitas*. It is almost a magic word, like *mysterium* in the writings of some authors. Under cover of the word, may not one fear a certain tendency to assert an independence in regard to the Holy Father?[37]

He told Mgr Dino Staffa, who had spoken in the same debate, that he could not accept the notion of *collegialitas episcoporum* except in the full Roman sense, '… a total dependence, in essence and in actuality, on the successor of Peter, the Roman Pontiff as defined in Vatican I'.[38]

Archbishop McQuaid realised after the Council that he had less support at the Irish Episcopal Conference and seemed disillusioned when replying in 1967 to Cardinal Conway's requests for comments on the Synod [of Bishops, in Rome] programme: 'Mine will be brief, and they will have no effect on the ultimate decision.'[39]

He was disappointed in 1970 when, after agreeing to remove the ban on Catholics attending Trinity College, Dublin, the hierarchy passed a resolution that a chaplain be appointed to the College. He saw this as ceding a bargaining point that could be used in further negotiations with Trinity and, among his notes, probably for an intervention at the continuation of the bishops' meeting next day, he wrote that:

> such a resolution passed by this assembly in effect forces the Archbishop of Dublin to take a certain step within his own Diocese. It will be the first occasion on which the Episcopal Conference will have forced a measure on an individual bishop.[40]

Diocesan Council of Priests

One outcome of collegiality was the introduction of diocesan councils of priests to participate in the running of dioceses. Mgr MacMahon sees it as another example of McQuaid's 'diligence' that he appointed one in Dublin before most other dioceses. Mgr Jerome Curtin also sees it as 'an important development' and an indication that the archbishop wanted to implement the Council. Dublin's first Council of Priests was appointed for three years, but the next one was, for the most part, elected. The function of the new Council, October 1966, was '… to implement the *Decree On the Ministry and Life of Priests* and the Motu Proprio, *Ecclesiae Sanctae*, No 15, which was issued by Pope Paul on August 6, 1966'. The purpose was 'to give, by its advice, effective assistance to the bishop in ruling the diocese'. It was to have 'merely a consultative voice' and the manner and forms of its working were to be determined by the bishop.[41]

Several priests, when asked, did not remember the first Council of Priests, or remembered it but thought it was ineffective. For Mgr Conor Ward, it was 'symbolic and useful to have' but its decisions 'did not impinge' on him very much. Mgr Tom Stack is doubtful what the first one, or even the second one, would have meant to the archbishop. He says no matter who was the chairman, he 'would have regarded it as a plaything. He was headmaster and he knew what was best.' Mgr MacMahon recognises the role of the Council of Priests in implementing Vatican II in the diocese, and suggests that 'some of them would have liked a faster pace, a more accelerated pace of reform'. Fr Gaughan believes there was disappointment among some priests because it was only consultative: 'You were simply consulted and it could be ignored.'

Parish councils

Parish councils, with laity and priests sharing in parish management and administration, were seen as collegiality at parish level. The bishops' June 1969 meeting recommended that parish councils be 'considered at an early date by Diocesan Councils of Priests, that the number of pilot schemes be extended and that where members are elected that the elections be by written vote'. The next meeting, November 1969, noted that progress in setting up councils had not been rapid enough but they 'could become purely formal structures making little real contribution to the Christian life of a parish'.[42]

Archbishop McQuaid was criticised for the slow introduction of parish councils in Dublin. Bishop Murray remembers there were 'few enough' of them in the 1960s. When one enthusiastic young priest informally gathered groups of young people from around the parish, his parish priest stopped him: 'You haven't a right to go and do this.' Fr Gaughan still sees a problem in the wrong sort of people being attracted to parish councils. His experience is that 'some would be merely interested in discussion rather than helping in a practical way with the running of the parish'. Mgr Fehily expresses a similar difficulty, but another senior parish priest says his parish is fully managed by a lay committee. Joe Fitz-Patrick says there were some councils in

Archbishop McQuaid's time but his parish priest told him: 'We don't need that'.

When Osmond Dowling saw a newspaper reference to Edenmore parish and a complaint that the parish council was overcharging for the use of the parish hall,[43] he expressed surprise to Mgr MacMahon, as he had not been aware there was a parish council in Edenmore. There was, as far as he knew, only one parish with such an organisation, Marino, 'and that what Canon Kelly had there was in fact not a full-scale parish council but a parish working party'. Mgr MacMahon shared Dowling's surprise but said it was possible there were parish councils in the diocese, although 'it was made clear at the last Diocesan Retreat that these Councils were not to be set up at present, without reference to the archbishop'.[44]

Catechesis and preaching
After the Council there were changes in catechesis, methods of religious instruction, both for schools and adults. Archbishop McQuaid moved quickly, commissioning a laywoman, Mary Purcell, to write *The Word of Truth*, a new series of three texts for primary schools in the Dublin diocese. Cardinal Conway, in a covering note to his discussion paper in 1969, 'Ireland in the Seventies', said:

> My impression is that the new programmes and methods now being used in the *primary* schools with the *On Our Way* series or the series by Mary Purcell, have been very successful and mark a distinct improvement on the older 'Catechism by Rote' method.

However, he did not have the same impression about post primary schools and there was 'a great need for a competent study in depth in this field'. He saw it as 'a most sensitive field...'[45]

There was dissatisfaction with some of the early drafts of new texts circulated by the Post-Primary Religious Texts Commission and one of Archbishop McQuaid's last letters was from Bishop Cahal Daly, then of Ardagh & Clonmacnoise, Chairman of the Episcopal Commission on Catechetics. McQuaid may have already complained, or Daly might have been anticipating complaint, when he wrote that he was 'seriously dissatisfied with some of the contents of the booklets hitherto distributed', but that 'none of the material was shown to me in advance of printing and distribution'.[46]

Before the Council, there was a fixed programme of topics about the basic doctrines of the church which priests preached at Sunday Mass. By 1970 it had been replaced by the homily drawn from the scriptural readings for the Mass of the day. Fr Butler says 'homilies are lovely', but catechesis is needed and he believes this was McQuaid's view also. He doesn't think McQuaid was happy with the new religious instruction after the Council and that for him, 'the catechism would last for another while and as the decrees of the Council were put into practice, then the catechism could be brought up to speed'.

Mgr Corish regrets the 'near collapse of catechesis', believing that while there were things in the old catechism, inherited from the Council of Trent, that needed re-thinking, it had value in that the key concepts sank in through repetition in a way that does not happen with children nowadays.

Joseph Foyle sees deterioration in preaching as a 'default effect' of the Council, which happened even if not intended: 'Previously the sermon could pick an issue over a period and keep reminding us of the basis of this and that. The homilies became totally banal and boring.' Foyle says the new preaching removed the devil and stopped talking about mortal sin and hell, and even purgatory, as a result of which people were no longer afraid. Foyle holds that McQuaid didn't but could have focused 'tightly on his own clergy' to get them 'preaching properly in a co-ordinated way'. Fr Gaughan agrees on a decline in preaching and in catechesis but also says, 'in fairness to the Council', it was not intended. He says the Council was balanced but people 'developed things out of it that it never intended'. He says the decline in the teaching of religion in school and in preaching has led to a whole generation that has to a considerable extent 'lost consciousness of sin, or wrongdoing, or immoral activity'. Fr Butler considers hell and damnation as only one aspect, but 'I think the clergy, we, have failed a bit in giving the doctrine of the church to the people ... if there was a little catechesis, just a little, at every Mass every Sunday ... the faith would be fine.'

While some nostalgia for the old style catechetical instruction and preaching still remains, the Public Image Committee report in 1964 found less enthusiasm and recommended change. They referred to a view expressed to them by lay people that 'you never hear a good sermon in our parish' and commented:

> The impact of the Council has made the laity more interested in developments in scripture, dogmatic and pastoral theology. They are better informed, and more inclined to look for precise information and guidance from their clergy. It is difficult for priests to be up to date and confident.
>
> Priests express great dissatisfaction with the programme of catechetical instruction. A special commission on this point, especially in the light of Constitution on the Liturgy, may be necessary.[47]

In those early years after the Council there were frequent criticisms of traditional preaching, with many of the laity acknowledging its influence upon them to be 'negligible' and often bearing no relevance to life as they knew it. The long, old-style, denunciatory sermon was going but, especially in vast city parishes, the sermon was too often composed as if there were only children present. However, there was one parish, St Michael and St John, on the Dublin City quays, where 3,000 people of all ages, from all sections of society, crowded in every week to listen in hushed silence to Fr Jack Whelan. It was 'the old message of the gospel, as new and as true today as ever, but it is the way he tells it that makes people come.'[48]

The bishops were worried. The Episcopal Commission on Doctrine, June 1968, reported:

> The Sunday homily on the gospel or liturgy does not lend itself easily to sustained and systematic exposition of the doctrines of the faith. It is urgently necessary that ways be found of reinstating the sort of coherent and continuous doctrinal and moral instruction, which used to be the aim of diocesan programmes of Catechetical Instruction.[49]

CHAPTER SIX

The Empty Chair –
Ecumenism in Dublin

Soon after Archbishop McQuaid's silver jubilee as archbishop, 27 December 1965, it was announced that, in January, during the annual Week of Prayer for Christian Unity (Church Unity Octave), he would join the Church of Ireland archbishop, George Otto Simms, in the Mansion House, Dublin, for a public lecture on ecumenism. This was welcomed with surprise, and interest grew after a report in *The Irish Times* that the two archbishops would sit together in the front row and say The Lord's Prayer with the audience. Although there then seemed to be some doubt about the prayer in common, the event suggested that McQuaid was embracing change. Fr Roland Burke Savage, not Osmond Dowling, organised the event. The lecturer was Mgr Arthur Ryan from Queen's University, Belfast, a senior priest remembered now by Fr Michael Hurley as a pre-Vatican II Catholic but respected as an ecumenist 'in general terms'. Seven hundred people attended the meeting and one writer has contrasted it favourably with the exclusion of Protestants from the Patrician Congress celebrations five years previously.[1] It is vividly remembered now after more than 40 years, not for what Mgr Ryan said, but for the confusion in the seating arrangements. When Archbishop McQuaid mounted the platform with Mgr Ryan and the Papal Nuncio, an empty chair remained beside them. The *Irish Press* reported other dignitaries, including President de Valera, Archbishop Simms, the Lord Mayor and the Chief Justice arriving at the front of the hall and finding they had no seats. James Dillon, a senior politician, offered his seat to the President and it was accepted with a smile, while ushers rushed to find seats for the others. What has lived in popular folklore has been the symbolism, or lack of it, of the 'empty chair'.

The Irish Times said the meeting was well-meant but oversold and the 'definite indication that the two Archbishops of Dublin would sit side by side raised hopes too much'. The editorial writer regretted an 'opportunity for a gesture of warmth and grace beyond the call of obvious ecclesiastical duty was missed'. The audience, with the two archbishops, recited The Lord's Prayer and *The Irish Catholic Directory* saw this climax as 'a direct implementation of the *Decree on Ecumenism* in which it is expressly stated that '... prayers may be recited in common with non-Catholics'.[3] For many, however, 'The Empty Chair' came to symbolise their spontaneous memory and perception of Archbishop McQuaid and ecumenism, just as the 'No Change' address symbolised McQuaid and the Council.

John Horgan remembers that people blamed McQuaid but 'the blame more properly resided with Burke Savage ... plainly it was a public relations disaster ... McQuaid would have recognised that ... I am sure that Simms himself, personally, took no offence.' Fr Michael Hurley also attributes a lot of the blame to Fr Burke Savage. Louis McRedmond immediately 'found it grossly and appallingly embarrassing'. He was sitting beside Douglas Gageby, editor of *The Irish Times* who, with a smile, told him this would mean six months of letters to his paper and so the phrase 'The Empty Chair' was coined.

McRedmond finds this typical of McQuaid trying to 'get in on the gesture' but thinks it ran 'slap up against his own scrupulosity, that he felt he was the Archbishop of Dublin and could not bring himself to put the other man up there on an equal par with himself'. He believes McQuaid knew 'the contumely that this would bring upon him, but it wouldn't stop him from doing it'. David Sheehy suggests he realised what had happened, but lacked the spontaneity to bring Simms up, and nobody else would dare do so. Patrick Masterson remembers how 'It turned out to be a bit chaotic ... and, of course, it created a *cause célèbre.*'

Fr Burke Savage's letter to McQuaid, in November, seems to have been the first proposal for the meeting: 'Would you think of allowing the Centre of Religious Studies and Information, of which you are the founder, to run a series of lectures in the Mansion House during the Church Unity Octave to which both

Catholics and our separated brethren could be invited ...'
McQuaid refused the project as 'premature', saying

> ... We as a hierarchy must await the *Directorium Generale*
> [Directory on Ecumenism] and then must ourselves elabo-
> rate a *Directorium* for our own circumstances. Neither
> *Directorium* has even been adumbrated. I may not then antic-
> ipate the decisions of my fellow bishops, even by a 'dramatic
> Christian (I would say Catholic) gesture' ... Be certain that
> relatively few educated people understand Oecumenism.
> Ordinary people are merely ignorant or confused.[5]

When Fr Burke Savage modified his proposal, McQuaid
replied:

> Your imagination is afire ... I do not want my Jubilee to be
> signalised by a celebration on Ecumenism. Cannot you do as
> I suggested? Have a set of clear talks in which Rev Hurley SJ
> will not figure – anywhere you wish on what the Decree
> means.[6]

Fr Burke Savage then sent, for McQuaid's approval, names of
speakers for the lectures. McQuaid objected:

> ... Are we so barren in Dublin, that we must search out aliens
> ... Mr Justice Kenny does not at all suggest himself: he is not
> clear, and is therefore not able to clear up others ... Fr
> McGarry [Editor, *The Furrow*] publicly criticised me for ap-
> pointing parish priests at 62 years. An arm-chair administra-
> tor, with no pastoral care ... Dr [Cecil] McGarry [Jesuit
> Rector] no. Dr Daly [the future Cardinal] no ... Give us
> Dublin. Mgr A. Ryan [Belfast] is very good and a gentleman'.

Nor did he want Fr Witte SJ, from the Gregorian University
in Rome, 'never heard of him', nor Dom Joseph Dowdall, Abbot
of Glenstal, nor Michael Gill ('too, too young') nor again J. G.
McGarry ('he castigated me publicly'). He placed a question
mark opposite Cecil McGarry. Among replacement names he
wanted Mgr Frank Cremin and Mgr Cecil Barrett.[7]

McQuaid finally decided: '... You should be content with a
Benediction in each parish church, with the prayer for unity, and
with one lecture, by Mgr A. Ryan on Tues 18th, with the Nuncio

presiding. I shall attend'.[8] There was humour in a further letter on 11 January: 'You are down an octave since I last saw you ... Could you please invite Rev Dr Cremin, Maynooth to your Tuesday affair. With kind hope that you will keep still down an octave.'[9] He was getting ready for the scapegoating by distancing himself from 'your Tuesday affair'. There is no reference to Archbishop Simms in the correspondence.

His next letter of 14 January was headmasterly:

> ... I have read with dismay the report in today's *Irish Times* of [next] Tuesday's meeting. It is an altogether unauthorised report. I am obliged to apologise to the Apostolic Nuncio for this report. You will take it as a formal, most formal expression of my will that you must never again make any mention of the archbishop on a published statement, without having first submitted to me that statement in writing.[10]

This was the report that the two archbishops would pray the Our Father together at the meeting.

McQuaid wrote again, same date, as Fr Burke Savage had delivered his reply immediately by hand:

> In view of the incredible statement attributed to you in the *Evening Press* you will understand that no one except Mr O. G. Dowling is authorised by me to issue any statement concerning the Tuesday meeting, either before Tuesday or on Tuesday or after Tuesday.[11]

And again, 16 January:

> If you have any queries about seating, you can discuss the matter with Doctor MacMahon. I shall sit on the right of the Apostolic Nuncio on the platform ... For what you should say, your text should first be passed by the Apostolic Nuncio who is chiefly concerned.

On the day after the meeting, he thanked Fr Burke Savage:

> Last night's lecture was widely appreciated to an extent that surprised me greatly, in view of its technical character. I thank you for the pains you took to achieve the result which gave so many persons an accurate account of Ecumenism.[12]

He made no reference to Archbishop Simms, nor the empty chair, nor the embarrassment arising out of the confusion over seating.

Two days later the letters to *The Irish Times* were in full flow. Osmond Dowling told McQuaid: 'The correspondence in *The Irish Times* on the Mansion House lecture continues. I do not have to reassure Your Grace that, despite repeated enquiries from the newspapers, we are not making any comment on the affair.' McQuaid noted: 'You make no answer whatever to anyone.'[13]

John Cooney has revealed a letter from McQuaid to Archbishop Simms' wife, Mercy, in April 1966, acknowledging that she and her husband must have suffered because of the Mansion House affair. Blaming Fr Burke Savage, McQuaid said, 'If we had set out to be discourteous and hurtful, a more sure result could not have been secured – all because of a good man's failure to coordinate and organise.' McQuaid claimed to have known nothing of the press releases and 'nothing about the empty chair', adding that he himself 'did not know too well' which chair he was meant to take.[14]

Fr Burke Savage remained upset at the manner in which McQuaid was blaming him, writing, 30 September 1966:

> Had I been keen on saving my own skin, I could have called off the meeting by a notice in the paper. I thought this would do Your Grace harm and so I went ahead in the full knowledge that I would be booted on all sides. I preferred to be the whipping boy because of regard and loyalty to you …
>
> Without ever asking for an explanation or of giving me a chance to offer any explanation, Your Grace formally denounced me to my own Provincial, and subsequently, I have good reason to believe, had a formal letter read at the Conferences in the diocese which put all the blame on me.[15]

The reply was sharp:

> … You are convinced that the 'Greek Tragedy' was caused by my failure to see you. Without attempting to sift for you the accuracy or inaccuracy of your beliefs, I shall be content to say that I am sorry for any fault I committed in all that period.

> I regret that I cannot accept your statement that I formally denounced you to your Provincial and, subsequently, *sine nomine* in a formal letter read to my clergy. I dealt not with the individual, nor with the local Superior, as is my practice, but with the major Superior, in a grave matter of public policy. Your description of my statement concerning the Mansion House meeting read to the clergy is not accurate ...
>
> I thank you for the gratitude and loyalty that you have so often expressed and I trust that I have your prayers.[16]

The two archbishops came together for another Church Unity Octave meeting in January 1967. This one was organised by Fr Liam Carey, Director of Dublin Institute of Adult Education (as Dublin Institute of Catholic Sociology had been re-named), in the National Stadium, Dublin. Archbishop McQuaid entered with Archbishop Simms and sat beside him throughout.[17] Mgr Patrick Boylan, a senior Dublin priest and biblical scholar, gave the lecture. Dr Patrick Masterson read a second paper, in response, and says he took 'a more philosophical approach to ecumenism and tried to locate it in the context of the greater unification that was going on around the world generally'. He believes McQuaid clearly made an effort to be as 'ecumenical as the matter allowed'. This meeting did not receive the same publicity as the Mansion House affair, and many of the interviewees do not remember it, possibly because it was non-controversial.

Ecumenism

Mgr Patrick J. Hamell, Vice-President, Maynooth College, gave a conservative, Catholic view of ecumenism on the eve of Vatican II:

> The ecumenical movement can be described briefly as what non-Catholics are doing to foster Christian unity ... Catholics do not take part in it, but follow it with sympathy and interest and have occasionally attended ecumenical gatherings as observers and have been received with the greatest courtesy.[18]

Tommy Commins, Irish Ambassador to the Holy See, emphasised the importance of ecumenism at the Council, telling Hugh McCann, Secretary, Department of External Affairs, that, despite the emphasis at the third session on the role of bishops, '... the theme of Ecumenism remained all pervading and, apart altogether from the individual *Schema* on Ecumenism, coloured consideration of all the other *Schemata* in more or less degree'.[19]

Archbishop McQuaid established, in 1963, a Centre of Religious Studies and Information with Fr Burke Savage as Director. It was first envisaged as similar to the London Catholic Enquiry Centre where non-Catholics could come for information about the Catholic Church, but by the time it started it was further intended to help lay people understand theology and matters emerging from Vatican II. In approving speakers for evening lectures in early 1965, McQuaid asked Fr Burke Savage to inform the press about the Centre, but 'emphasise its establishment by me last year – lest it be confused as an ecumenical gesture'. Fr Burke Savage saw no need to point out that the gestation period was so long, but McQuaid replied: 'I should prefer to take more responsibility for the Centre venture than you kindly allow – come what may from our efforts ...' He wanted it understood that the scheme was not modern nor, 'as it is being suggested, another measure of *aggiornamento* wrung from the archbishop by the criticism of journalists and others'.[20] There was such a large attendance at the first lecture of a series on 'Understanding the Liturgy', given by Mgr Michael O'Connell, that it had to be repeated.[21]

While Archbishop McQuaid 'did not tell his people that the *aggiornamento* was a good thing or a bad thing',[22] it was clear that he did not like it. The word, literally meaning updating or modernisation, was introduced by Blessed John XXIII to convey the purpose of Vatican II. McQuaid shared his thoughts with Bishop Browne of Galway when he praised the Holy Faith nuns: 'They will do anything to aid a parish priest. They are untouched by modern craze for *aggiornamento*.'[23]

He was criticised for being anti-ecumenical in his attitude to mixed marriages. He did what he could to prevent them and then prescribed regulations that were stricter than in other dioceses and humiliating to the non-Catholic partner. The Public Image Committee (1964) reproached him:

The rules in this archdiocese for the celebration of Mixed

Marriages are an embarrassment to any priest who has to commend them to a couple ... While having no doubt about the undesirability of mixed marriages, the Commission [Committee] respectfully recommend that, when permission is given for such marriages, they should be celebrated with good grace.[24]

A draft *Directory on Ecumenism*, prepared in Rome, under Augustin Cardinal Bea and the Secretariat for Promoting Christian Unity, was sent to Cardinal Conway in 1966. It was marked '*sub secreto*' – only the bishops knew about it at this stage. McQuaid's comments, purporting, as always, to represent the views of 'our people', were very strong as regards the special circumstances of ecumenism in Dublin:

... ecumenism is with us in Dublin, a gravely delicate process, which requires careful preparation and very tactful execution ... It cannot be hastened, no matter what a minimal group may urge ... For what concerns spiritual ecumenism: our people will readily agree to pray for the conversion of non-Catholics. For what concerns spiritual participation: our people take a very different attitude ... Par 37(b) could be a grave scandal [It refers to possibility of church buildings being shared in some circumstances] ... I should like to see very firmly safeguarded the rights of the local bishop to judge the suitability of ecumenical efforts in his own territory ... It must be emphasised that relations, social, professional and cultural, between Catholics and non-Catholics are in this diocese quite charitable. Non-Catholics have very frequently acknowledged the charity and justice uniformly shown them.[25]

He added a final, handwritten paragraph inserted (presumably) before the letter was typed and sent to Bishop Donal Herlihy, Secretary of the Hierarchy Commission on Ecumenism: 'Cardinal Bea is a zealous man but he is not the Archbishop of Dublin where the situation needs very delicate handling.'

The hierarchy meeting, June 1966, decided Catholics could now attend weddings, baptisms and funerals of non-Catholic friends, including being best man or bridesmaid at weddings; elected representatives and public officials could attend non-Catholic services in the course of their civic duties, and Catholics could attend common services like those organised for Remembrance Day. McQuaid had not been happy when this was first suggested and his note, on a letter from Bishop Herlihy, invoked his 'people' once more: 'Thank you. It will take a deal of explaining to *my* people.'[26]

Louis McRedmond believes that 'the whole ecumenical exercise was very much welcomed in Ireland at the time at the level of gesture', and that it never really advanced beyond that. While the question of praying together, but not sharing each other's liturgical services, became accepted, 'what was of course much slower off the ground was any theological approach'. He points encouragingly, to the annual Greenhills Conference which started in the late 1960s and the founding of the Irish School of Ecumenics in 1970, and says: 'These were important, serious attempts at ecumenism ... and I would still feel that the Catholic bishops in Ireland were very edgy about these serious things. They were all for the gesture.'

Fr Michael Hurley also sees how McQuaid came to accept gestures in ecumenism and 'when he thought it right and proper he had no difficulty being ecumenically correct and exquisitely polite'. He recalls McQuaid's 1967 Dublin meeting with Archbishop Ramsey of Canterbury and refers to his willingness to 'acquiesce' in the setting up of the Irish School of Ecumenics and to 'acquiesce' in the launch of a major book on Irish Anglicanism.

Canon Paddy Battelle and Mgr Tom Fehily deny that Archbishop McQuaid was anti-Protestant, citing his friendship with Archbishop Simms and his wife, Mercy, as one example. According to Mgr Fehily, McQuaid never 'spoke disrespectfully' of a Protestant, maintaining there would never be trouble in talking to another person who also 'tried to practise their faith fully'. He told John H. Whyte he had no difficulty working with Protestants, one of many instances being when he brought in a prominent freemason to play a very active role in the Ballyowen TB sanatorium project in the 1940s.[27]

Mercy Simms proposed ideas to him that might have been more difficult through official channels, writing informally and, sometimes, apparently, without the knowledge of her husband. She thanked him in January 1967 for a book on the life of St

Teresa, and suggested, in relation to the forthcoming lectures in Dublin by Archbishop Ramsey:

> You would probably find it an embarrassment to attend either of these yourself, but any observer you might send would be most welcome. George hopes to arrange a meeting, if possible, for you both sometime during his weekend here.[28]

She suggested Unity Week, 1968, be marked

> with joint Bible readings, interspersed with sacred music by various choirs ending perhaps with the Apostle's Creed as well as the Lord's Prayer? Your people seem eager for joint prayer and also long for more personal contact with you. If you read a lesson, it could have a wonderful effect on them – the Stadium would not hold all who would want to come.

McQuaid's note: 'Thank you. Such a meeting would require much thought. Apparently the C of I [Church of Ireland] Gazette does not approve of my inviting you and His Grace.'[29]

Simms approached McQuaid for this meeting with Ramsey during his June visit and he replied that he would be 'honoured to meet with Dr Ramsey'. Simms then confirmed he would bring Ramsey to call on McQuaid.[30] The meeting at Archbishop's House, on 24 June 1967, was a success, with a press photocall and favourable coverage. For instance, the *Sunday Mirror* had a photograph of the three archbishops on page 1: 'The man who came to tea' and noted that 'the three church leaders drank tea and chatted for 30 minutes'. However, it took persuasion from Osmond Dowling for McQuaid to agree to the photocall and he was not pleased at being pushed.[31]

His apparent lack of shift in attitude to ecumenism was shown in frequent pastoral letters after the Council. In a January 1968 letter, he regretted that the faithful might be 'confused' by discussions during Church Unity Octave and

> ... induced to forget that the Octave is chiefly an occasion for humble prayer that God in His Mercy, by the intercession of Our Blessed Lady, may hasten the day when all Christians now unfortunately separated from the Holy See in Faith and discipline, may accept the one true Church of Christ.[32]

This was the letter which caused John Feeney to apologise to all other Christians for McQuaid's position. An *Irish Times* editorial said it would come as a considerable shock to 'many deeply-committed Christians' and commented: 'Dr McQuaid's letters, as most people in his diocese know, are read by fellow-Christians outside his own persuasion with perturbation and with sadness.'[33]

The *Church of Ireland Gazette* commented that McQuaid's conception of prayer for unity 'seems to be out of spirit with that of the Vatican Secretariat for Unity and is disappointing because it would make it difficult for all the followers of Christ to join in prayer for unity thus conceived.'[34]

In 1968, Seán MacRéamoinn read a lesson in St Patrick's [Church of Ireland] Cathedral in Dublin at an interdenominational service for Martin Luther King. He didn't believe he needed the archbishop's permission, but didn't want to be discourteous because it was unusual, 'probably the first time that a Roman Catholic had taken part in a service there since the time of King James II [17th century]'. So, afterwards, he rang Osmond Dowling to put it on the record. Dowling thanked him and he heard nothing more for some months until he rang Dowling about something else and Dowling said, 'I should have been in touch with you ... got a note from His Grace ... I should have passed it on to you'. MacRéamoinn remembers the note clearly: 'With regard to the participation by Mr Seán MacRéamoinn in a service in St Patrick's Cathedral'- and no reference to Martin Luther King – 'would you be kind enough to express my appreciation to Mr MacRéamoinn of his courtesy in informing me of this act, while deploring his action, which has caused widespread anxiety ...' MacRéamoinn laughs heartily as he recalls this: 'Widespread anxiety. All over Dublin!' The archives back up MacRéamoinn's accurate memory of this incident, which was taken very seriously in Archbishop's House. Mgr MacMahon told McQuaid:

> I commented to Mr Dowling that the discipline of the Liturgy in the diocese was of such importance that Mr MacRéamoinn left himself open to severe criticism by reading a lesson without permission; any integral judgement of the situation

should take account of the bishops' responsibility in this field.[35]

Archbishop McQuaid congratulated Simms on his election, in 1969, as Archbishop of Armagh but expressed 'deep regret' that he and his wife would leave Dublin. He wished them God's blessing in their 'new and difficult sphere' and 'for very many kindnesses and a very constant courtesy, I am indeed grateful'.[36]

Sean MacRéamoinn says Mercy Simms rang McQuaid to say farewell, as they were going to Armagh that evening, sooner than they had expected, and he said he would be around 'in a minute or two':

> And she said it was unlike him but he came around and spoke to both of them, and expressed great regret [that they were leaving Dublin]. And she walked down to the gate and he turned to her and said, 'somebody like me can only guess at the great value of the great service that a woman like yourself can do for a man in his position.

This suggests that Archbishop McQuaid's friendship with Archbishop Simms was more than a gesture. With the exception of one letter, it seems to have been a feature since Simms' appointment as archbishop in 1957, with regular exchanges of books and gifts.[37] It seems, however, to have developed only after Simms was appointed to Dublin from Cork. He had been Dean of Residence (chaplain) in Trinity College from 1939 to 1952. When Bishop William Philbin, then of Clonfert, asked McQuaid's views on whether he should speak to a Literary & Historical Society meeting in UCD, at which Simms was going to be present, McQuaid urged him to accept: 'Dr Simms, as I fully expected, is going to repeat his Cork tactics – attend everything, speak at everything. I shall take care of him quietly. His irruption into UCD, in view of his TCD background, will be a beginning of further worry.'[38]

It would be hard to believe that the apparently sincere friendship with Simms over his remaining years was just a strategy to 'take care of him quietly'.

Evidence of later change in McQuaid's attitude, not just to Archbishop Simms but to other dignitaries of the Church of Ireland, is clear in the courteous way he sent representatives to the consecration of their bishops – a gesture, and possibly only a gesture, but one that would have been sinful a few years before. Two examples were Dean Salmon of Christ Church Cathedral inviting a representative to the enthronement of their new Archbishop (Alan Buchanan) in succession to Simms. McQuaid replied: 'It is a pleasure to assure you that I have arranged with Mgr Hurley, VG to assist at the enthronement.' Again, in reply to Dean Salmon who asked the same for the consecration of Donald Caird as Bishop of Limerick, also in Christ Church Cathedral, he came back: 'Thank you for the courteous invitation. I have asked Mgr Hurley, Vicar General, to assist.'[39] This use of the word 'assist', rather than 'attend' can mean more than being just a passive observer at the ceremony.

McQuaid maintained clear limits on his ecumenical positions. His pastoral letter for Church Unity Octave in 1971, read at all Masses, stated unequivocally that 'only in the Catholic Church is found all the doctrine of Jesus Christ, unchanged and guaranteed to be unchanged, because of the infallibility that he personally bestowed upon the Pope, successor of St Peter, and upon his church in which the bishops are the lawful successors of the apostles'.[40]

Commenting that the Octave had 'begun on a rather frigid note for Catholics in the Archdiocese of Dublin', a *Sunday Independent* editorial claimed McQuaid wanted unity 'on his own terms', with the Protestants seeing the errors of their ways and rejoining the Catholic Church unconditionally, and added that his attitude towards Protestants had been 'consistent and always unequivocal – they are totally in error and that is an end of it'.[41]

Trinity College, Dublin

Discussion on Archbishop McQuaid's approach to ecumenism has to include the case of the University of Dublin, Trinity College, founded 1592. The Irish hierarchy, for many years, banned Catholic students, 'under pain of mortal sin', from attending Trinity College. The ban, in Statute 287 of the Plenary Council of Maynooth, was re-iterated periodically and stated: 'Only the Archbishop of Dublin is competent to decide circumstances in which attendance may be tolerated.' McQuaid's

Lenten Regulations, 1964, for example, stated: 'Attendance may be tolerated only for grave and valid reasons and with the addition of definite measures, by which it is sought to safeguard the faith and practice of a Catholic student.'[42] The ban was imposed and maintained by the hierarchy, not McQuaid, and for more than two hundred years before the ban, Trinity itself had barred Catholics. Maeve McRedmond accepts it was not McQuaid's idea, 'but, he certainly agreed with it!' He told John H. Whyte that people would not be so critical if they knew what happened to the applications for permission, and he gave a 'slight nod of his head' to indicate that most of them were granted.[43]

He took exception, in 1959, to Trinity raising funds in the USA and to F. H. Boland, Ireland's representative at the United Nations, and a Catholic, being a member of the fund-raising committee. He wrote to every bishop in the USA and Canada, with the agreement of Cardinal D'Alton and the hierarchy, condemning the project and including a long, polemical statement on the Irish University question.[44]

Fr Michael Hurley remembers his superiors, in 1962, indicating that, because of the archbishop's well-known stance on the matter, he should decline an invitation to address the Student Christian Movement (SCM) in Trinity on 'The Vatican Council and the Ecumenical Situation Today'. The meeting moved to a local hotel so that Fr Hurley could give the lecture. Joe Fitz-Patrick remembers a Dominican priest addressing a meeting during the campaign for nuclear disarmament, 'and all hell broke loose next day. Archbishop McQuaid wanted to know who allowed this man to go to Trinity: "He went in without my permission".' Fitz-Patrick attended Trinity with McQuaid's permission but he formed the opinion that Catholic students there were 'lepers' and totally 'ignored' by McQuaid.

The draft report of the Public Image Committee (1964) said Trinity remained a 'burning issue':

> ... the appeal to Canon law as justification is no longer convincing. Though many feel that we should solve the problem by 'flooding' Trinity College with Catholics, public opinion in general does not appear adverse to the law as such. However, public opinion does appear to discountenance the

annual repetition of the prohibition at such length. And public opinion seems to see the need for the appointment of a full-time chaplain, to safeguard the faith of the large number of Catholic students in Trinity, many of them with the permission of His Grace, many more from England and foreign countries ...'[45]

Mgr Frank Cremin, with Archbishop McQuaid's encouragement, delivered four talks in Trinity, on the Vatican Council, during Church Unity Octave, 1965. They were followed by questions, but not discussion, and he felt 'much had already been achieved when we arrived, as we so often did, at the hard core of differences between us and agreed to differ'.[46]

For the first time since 1944, probably influenced by the report of the Public Image Committee, McQuaid did not mention the Trinity ban in his 1965 or 1966 Lenten regulations, but it reappeared in 1967: 'The law passed by all the bishops of Ireland and confirmed by the Holy See has not been changed or relaxed. They who hear or read this authentic declaration cannot claim to act in good conscience when they violate this law.'[47]

The Irish Times commented twice on this resurgence of the Trinity issue, saying it was 'one of the festering sores in our community life'.[48] The *Sunday Independent* had re-published McQuaid's 1961 pastoral letter on *Higher Education for Catholics*, with its attack on Trinity, in feature article format, alongside a friendly editorial, 'Attacks on the Archbishop of Dublin'. McQuaid thanked the editor, Hector Legge, for 'the courage of your editorial yesterday and for your sense of justice as a Catholic'.[50]

The proposed UCD/Trinity merger which Donogh O'Malley, Minister for Education, announced some weeks later, hastened the end of the ban. There is a long, handwritten note by McQuaid about a meeting in May 1967 which began over lunch with himself, Bishop Michael Browne of Galway, Bishop William Philbin of Down & Connor, Jeremiah Hogan, President of UCD, and Michael Tierney, the former President. Hogan and Tierney withdrew at 3 pm and the bishops were joined by the Minister and Toirleach Ó Raifeartaigh, Secretary, Department of Education. McQuaid described the three-hour discussion with O'Malley and O Raifeartaigh as very open, very explicit and friendly ... The Minister thanks us, said he only wishes to do what we thought to be right and would gladly meet us as often as we wished. He could not have shown greater goodwill, good humour and realistic grasp of the difficult task before him.

The merger was soon floundering due to staff resistance and McQuaid did not want the bishops blamed but the process continued. He told Hogan of his conviction 'that the so-called merger is a morass of unsolved difficulties'.[51]

Bishop Browne told McQuaid of a later meeting of the National University of Ireland Senate in 1969 to consider and report on the new University Scheme, and how it agreed that 'the ban on Trinity would go but no explanation was given of how Trinity would change its identity, ethos and constitution and how the new University would be Christian'.[52] McQuaid replied:

> I am amazed at the statement that the ban would go. I never once gave Dr Ó Raifeartaigh the slightest hope that the ban could go until the bishops were completely satisfied that the nature and status of Trinity had been so radically and legally altered that they could accept the new arrangement ... I am the more grateful for Your Lordship's letter in that I have been kept in the dark.[53]

The Trinity ban was finally lifted in June 1970. It was announced from the hierarchy meeting:

> ... Some hope for a change that would make this institution acceptable to the Catholic conscience was provided by the announcement of a proposed merger of Trinity College and University College, Dublin ... In view of the substantial agreement on basic issues that has been reached by the National University of Ireland and Trinity College, the hierarchy has decided to seek approval from the Holy See for repeal of Statute 287 of the Plenary Synod.[54]

Archbishop McQuaid's copy of the minutes includes a handwritten note that the Trinity statement was passed by 18 votes to 8. The bishops also passed a resolution that a chaplaincy be set up. McQuaid did not see why 'at this moment precisely, we should wish to urge the establishment of a chaplaincy. There is no immediate compelling reason. On the contrary a resolution calling on me to establish a chaplaincy is very badly timed, in my opinion.'[54]

CHAPTER SEVEN

The Aftermath –
Dream Destroyed or Just Delayed?

Pope Paul VI, in his encyclical, *Humanae Vitae* (of Human Life), published on 29 July 1968, confirmed the Catholic Church's long-standing ban on all artificial methods of contraception. He had removed contraception from discussion at the Council and appointed a Pontifical Commission on Population, Family and Birth to report to him. The Commission sat for two years and its report, made public in 1967, proposed that birth regulation by artificial methods might, in certain circumstances, be made acceptable. His decision to reject the Commission's report took many by surprise and resulted in unease throughout the church, with public rejection of the encyclical by certain laity, clergy and even bishops.

David Rice, then a priest in the Dominican order, claims *Humanae Vitae* was 'one of the greatest hoaxes of the 20th century, that the Pope then came out and condemned contraception not because he believed it was wrong but because he didn't want the church to look bad'. Rice's view is shared by others who spoke and wrote at the time and afterwards. Fr Gabriel Daly OSA sees *Humanae Vitae* as 'a highly symbolic act concerned more with church authority than with the substantive moral issues it dealt with'.[1]

Fr Seán Fagan comments on how the Commission voted almost unanimously for change. Only four of its 72 clerical and lay members voted against change and those four were priests. They admitted that their position could not be proved, but claimed that changing the teaching would cause a schism in the church. They wrote this to Pope Paul VI and continued to play on his fears as he prepared the encyclical. The Pope later said this was the worst period of his life, and he had to live with it. The tenour of this perspective is backed up by others, including Robert B. Kaiser.[2]

For one Dublin parish priest, now retired, *Humanae Vitae* was 'a crushing blow' and induced 'a tremendous sense of depression'. He was visiting a seminary for lunch and one of the priests arrived late to say he had just heard that the Pope had forbidden any kind of artificial contraception, any change in the church law: 'And you could hear a pin drop. And two men stood up and walked out, while another one or two were positively gloating.' Fr Dermod McCarthy says Fr Kevin McNamara, Professor of Moral Theology at Maynooth, and later Archbishop of Dublin, was so convinced there would be change that he had prepared documentation for his students to justify the theological reasons for it.

Archbishop McQuaid's press conference

A Dublin press conference to introduce and explain the encyclical was held at Mater Dei Institute. Opening it, Archbishop McQuaid expressed 'confident belief that this official teaching of the church will find in the mind and heart of the priests entrusted to my pastoral care the response of an immediate renewal of loyalty to the church'. He then left, while Mgr Frank Cremin conducted the conference which, he said, was arranged by the Holy See with the archbishop providing the facilities.[3] Joe Power says McQuaid told Mgr Cremin before he left Rome that he wanted him in Dublin, 'the morning after next', to do the press conference.

Louis McRedmond, then editor of the *Irish Independent*, was in attendance. He says there was a detailed summary, prepared by Mgr Cremin, but not the full text of the encyclical. Joe Power recalls about 'half a dozen questions' afterwards but then 'Mgr Cremin was so fulsome in what he said, we didn't need elaboration, I mean he had it all in script form, and most journalists took the easy way out'. John Horgan says Mgr Cremin spoke for nearly an hour, uninterrupted: 'The journalists were there with their jaws hanging open, wondering what on earth was going on … it was a harangue.' Joseph Foyle remembers journalists 'snorting because the Pope wasn't changing to their liking. And they were stuck with the fact that there was no change. And you could feel the atmosphere … And then, *non licet*, no change.' Foyle says 'Poor old Cremin was above being pilloried, and

Paddy Gallagher [an RTÉ television reporter] was huffing and puffing about lack of compassion in this treatment of unfortunate people' and Mgr Cremin could only reply: 'How do you say "no" nicely?'

An *Irish Times* appreciation on Mgr Cremin's death in 2001 stated he was 'by conviction, not conditioning,' consistently against contraception both before and after the encyclical and his typical question was: if the church changed her mind on this vital issue, 'which was the true church – the one that had opposed contraception or the one that now accepted it?'[4] This would seem to have been Archbishop McQuaid's dilemma also, as with other issues such as ecumenism – if it was a sin to pray with Protestants before Vatican II and not now, had the church's teaching been false? Which church was to be believed?

Louis McRedmond had arranged to receive the full text of the encyclical through a contact in the Papal Nunciature, so he left the press conference early to return to his office for it. When he left, 'in the corridor outside was a very anxious John Charles pacing up and down, all by himself'. McRedmond said: 'Your Grace, Dr Cremin, he is having to bat on a pretty heavy wicket at the moment in there', to which the archbishop replied: 'A brilliant man, Dr Cremin, Mr McRedmond, and will he be finished soon?' McQuaid used criticise Rome for releasing important information to the press before telling bishops, but he commented to Cardinal Conway: '*Humanae Vitae*, in the manner of its release, was, in general, a distinct improvement.'[5]

The Archbishop assures the Pope

McQuaid sent an immediate telegram to Cardinal Cicognani, Secretary of State, 'on behalf of the clergy and the faithful of the Archdiocese of Dublin, and on my own part'. He welcomed the Pope's 'reaffirmation of the constant doctrine of the church on marriage' and gave assurance of 'our total acceptance of his official teaching'.[6] Cardinal Cicognani replied that the Pope thanked him for 'the message of loyalty and support'.[7] McQuaid again had *Humanae Vitae* in mind two years later when he congratulated the Pope on the silver jubilee of his priesthood and assured him of the fidelity of the Dublin priests and laity to his teachings:

It must be for the Holy Father a deep consolation to know that not a single priest of this diocese has, by word or writing, failed fully to respect the teaching of the Pope on faith and morals.

The faithful, too, for all the pressure of evil and all the influences of the mass media, remain in very greatest proportion, true to the faith, and the practice of the faith, especially to Holy Mass and Holy Communion.[8]

Irish bishops and Humanae Vitae

A statement from the Irish Episcopal Conference saw the encyclical as 'the authoritative teaching of the Pope' and they were confident the people would 'accept it as such and give it that wholehearted assent which the Second Vatican Council requires'. They said the Pope did not speak as 'one theologian among many but as the Vicar of Christ who has the special assistance of the Holy Spirit in teaching the universal church'. The statement called for study and prayer and for priests in confession to show 'understanding and sympathy', but 'without compromise of principle'.[9]

Dublin priests and Humanae Vitae

Fr Austin Flannery believes Dublin priests 'kept ranks' over *Humanae Vitae*. Fr Seán Fagan says they were 'upset'. Fr Eltin Griffin remembers that some of them were 'very uneasy about it'. Fr Tony Gaughan does not believe priests 'had a difficult time' because 'people made up their own minds and were sensible about it, but the man at the top had to lay down the principle'. For Fr Dermod McCarthy, *Humanae Vitae* was the 'most unfortunate papal document of the latter half of the twentieth century' and caused 'huge' problems for priests. He tried to implement it in the confession boxes, 'with little sense of loyalty to it ... no sense of belief that I was doing the right thing ... trying to find loopholes ... to find ways out of the actual letter of the law ...' He believes it accounted for many of the priests who afterwards left ministry: 'They decided not to go public on this in a confrontational way. They just decided to leave...'

Canon Paddy Battelle admits that *Humanae Vitae* was a problem and it led to priests leaving the ministry. Fr Griffin believes it was a major factor in disturbing both laity and priests: 'All hell was let loose. And a lot of laity left the church at that time ... And the number of priests who left Dublin after Vatican II was frightening, there must have been a hundred priests who left.' Despite this impression, very few Dublin priests resigned during Archbishop McQuaid's episcopacy. In response to a Catholic Communications Institute survey in 1971, he replied that the numbers of Dublin priests who had left in the previous five years were: 1966 – 0; 1967 – 2; 1968 – 1; 1969 – 4; 1970 – 3.[10] Editions of the *Irish Catholic Directory*, 1971 through 1977, show that, afterwards, the number of priests of the diocese, including retired priests, dropped from 603 to 550, with ordinations exceeding deaths by 10. This, assuming the accuracy of these figures, shows a drop of up to 63 in six years.

Laity and Humanae Vitae

Mgr Patrick Corish believes *Humanae Vitae*, for the laity, was 'badly handled'. It was a 'marking point' because it was central to their lives, but 'it was presented in terms of a theology where everything was forbidden and nearly everything was mortal sin'. Louis McRedmond sees it as the first time bishops had to defend themselves against their laity. One parish priest remembers 'a lot of people had dilemmas and talked about it. And it was through lay people that I began to feel this is wrong and that we shouldn't be so rigid in these things'. He says he could not ever be 'rigid' in confession or when otherwise counselling people as to their practices about contraception, but he worried about it, and 'everybody knew that there was that report, that it was only a minority who favoured against changing'.

Dermot Keogh believes many Irish people 'simply chose to ignore the official church teaching' and to use 'artificial means' of birth control, although for some it meant their consciences 'forced them to leave the church'. For others, 'loyalty to church teaching was paramount'.[11] Keogh's judgement is that the encyclical challenged the laity to 'think for themselves and become, as a consequence, more independent of hierarchical structures'. Louise Fuller makes a similar judgement in the context of the Council's emphasis on the primacy of conscience, saying many Irish Catholics 'appear to have decided that while the bishops might pronounce on issues of private morality they – the laity – were entitled to make up their own minds'.[12]

How Archbishop McQuaid handled the issue
Mgr Stephen Greene thinks the announcement and the press conference could have been handled in a 'more understanding way' and that Mgr Cremin 'was very much in tune with the mind of the church, so therefore you got it, and you either took it or you didn't ...' One parish priest, who would be quite liberal in his theology, gives Archbishop McQuaid 'some sort of credit' for the way he handled the issue and fallout from it, compared to certain bishops abroad, including his friend Patrick Cardinal O'Boyle, of Washington DC, who suspended 19 dissenting priests, with public controversy continuing for some years until the Vatican stepped in and calmed the storm. There was neither public sacking nor denunciation of priests in Dublin who did not support it fully. When it was issued, one priest, whom McQuaid asked to address meetings of priests in the diocese, re-members being verbally attacked, 'about to be devoured', by a large, elderly parish priest when he said dissent from the non-infallible teaching of the Pope was accepted in Catholic theology. He says McQuaid knew about this but he was never reprimanded. Canon Battelle agrees McQuaid did not adopt a line of public reprimands for priests who seemed to be out of line, but 'he would have spoken quietly to them'. Fr Gaughan says it was a very hard issue to 'handle properly' but praises McQuaid who was 'at the top of the pyramid' and had to set it out 'in black and white'. Lower down there was more flexibility and he himself would say to people: 'Do the best you can.' Fr Tom Butler says McQuaid never spoke to him about *Humanae Vitae*, but believes it 'was a great trial' for him and 'it distressed him greatly that people would blatantly and openly go against the teaching of the Pope'.

Garret FitzGerald, later Taoiseach, and his wife, Joan, were at a Wexford conference, in September 1968, to discuss the encyclical. The conference issued a report on problems the encyclical created for a significant number of people. Vincent Grogan, Supreme Knight of St Columbanus, on the participants' behalf, circulated the report to the hierarchy. McQuaid replied: 'I thank you for your manifesto. I feel sure that you would prefer to go to your judgement with the knowledge that you had done all in your power to secure full assent to the teaching of the Vicar of Christ'.[13]

McQuaid supported Cardinal O'Boyle against his priests who rebelled over *Humanae Vitae*, but did not adopt similar tactics in Dublin. O'Boyle sent him a booklet on *Humanae Vitae* and he promised he would study it, praying 'that God may give you courage to withstand steadfastly the disobedience of priests'.[14] He also supported Bishop Cornelius Lucey of Cork & Ross who withdrew diocesan faculties for hearing confessions and for preaching from Fr James Good who went public on 'his deeply-felt conscientious objection to a non-infallible Papal Encyclical': 'You have come out of the Good affair very handsomely. Congratulations.'[15]

The Institute of Public Administration (IPA) asked Osmond Dowling to chair a debate on the proposition: 'That the people of Ireland should reject the terms of the Encyclical, *Humanae Vitae*.' He told the archbishop he had declined and McQuaid noted: 'You did well to refuse. The invitation was provocative and hurtful.' McQuaid immediately wrote to the Principal, IPA: 'I hereby formally protest, as Archbishop of Dublin, against a proposition that, in effect, suggests the apostasy of Catholics by the rejection of the explicit, authentic teaching of the Vicar of Christ.'[16]

The Media and Humanae Vitae

Louis McRedmond says *Humanae Vitae* 'did not get a very good run from the media in Ireland … it was all questioning, the editorials were questioning … there were as many critical articles as there were those that came out from predictable sources in support'. He remembers how Mgr Cremin, upset when he heard the *Irish Independent* was running the full text of the encyclical, rang him that evening and said the initial Latin text had some errors, but McRedmond assured him that a Latin scholar in the newspaper was checking that. An *Irish Independent* editorial believed such protest as had emerged in Ireland might be 'no more than the tip of an iceberg' with what the laity said in private going unrecorded and the clergy saying what they thought more often to their friends than to the newspapers.[17]

Erosion of public enthusiasm for Vatican II

Decline in enthusiasm for the Council is often traced to the *Humanae Vitae* controversy, the revolt of laity and priests against authority and then indications that the Vatican was trying to pull back on change. Louis McRedmond believes interest in the Council 'all changed' after *Humanae Vitae*: 'You didn't hear much more of meetings being organised around the country to explain aspects of Vatican II.' Maeve McRedmond doesn't quite agree that the 'great excitement' was really finished, and Louis concedes that *Humanae Vitae* '... didn't finish it, but it put a big crack in it which brought it down in the end ... The church authorities, I mean the bishops specifically, they closed ranks, they became suspicious of what was being written ...'

Joe Fitz-Patrick concedes there were 'cosmetic changes' like lay readers in the church, but for him the euphoria of the Council evaporated and 'a fog descended'. Looking back, one parish priest calls for more patience in a church which traditionally has thought in terms of centuries. He does not believe the Council can be submitted to a final judgement, even after forty years: 'Anything that happened in the church that was good, didn't happen suddenly. It was gradual. And I think that really it would be foolish for us to say the Vatican Council failed ...'

It may have been a sign that the conservatives were winning when Cardinal Conway told Archbishop McQuaid that the Synod of Bishops in Rome in 1969 'went well; no explosive proposals were pushed – I think those who might have been inclined to do so sensed that the general mood of the bishops was not propitious for their ideas'.[18] John Horgan reported the closure of *Herder Correspondence* and the comment of its editor, Robert Nowell, that it had 'fallen victim to the aftermath of Vatican II, to the era of disillusion, contestation and polarisation that has succeeded the euphoric hopefulness the Council was able to generate'.[19]

Vincent Grogan and the Knights of St Columbanus

The conservative/liberal polarity in the post-Council church affected McQuaid's dealings with some members of the Knights of St Columbanus. This lay Order was one of his favourite organisations and he built close personal friendships with several of its members, including Supreme Knights Dr J. Stafford Johnson and Dermot O'Flynn. He attended their meetings regularly, asked for and received their help in numerous charitable activities and used them as watchdogs in his campaigns against what he saw as evil and liberal tendencies.

This friendship did not extend to Vincent Grogan, the Dublin constitutional lawyer, who was elected Supreme Knight in June 1966. Grogan was well-known as a liberal and frequently appeared on television to express his views. It was not really a surprise when, at the banquet to celebrate his election, attended by Cardinal Conway, Grogan made a strong call for *aggiornamento*, efforts to create a more liberal and reforming agenda in the Order, and abolition of the relative secrecy which had traditionally surrounded their membership and their activities. He sent copies of his address to all of the bishops.

He wrote to McQuaid in August, presenting his 'respectful compliments' and seeking an opportunity to call on him. McQuaid instructed his secretary, Fr John Fitzpatrick, to reply: 'I am directed by HGAB [His Grace the Archbishop] to thank you for this first intimation of your election in June. On return from Lourdes, HG will arrange to see you.' Reference to 'first intimation' shows McQuaid was not pleased and it broke the traditional practice of writing personally to Supreme Knights.

Grogan wrote in September, after McQuaid's return from Lourdes:

> I know how fully occupied you are at present, and appreciate that it may be some time before you are free to see me. In the meantime, there is one matter of some urgency on my mind: The appointment of a Supreme Chaplain. It is the privilege of the Supreme Knight for the time being – subject to ecclesiastical approval – to nominate his Chaplain.
>
> I should very much like to invite Rev James Kavanagh to take the office. He is an old friend: we were at O'Connell School together …

McQuaid's noted: 'I agree.' Fr Fitzpatrick sent the reply to Grogan.

Grogan wrote thanking McQuaid for agreeing to Fr Kavanagh's appointment, followed by a further letter, Grogan stating that Fr

Kavanagh had accepted, but adding: 'He told me he was influenced by my address on the occasion of our Banquet, of which I believe Your Grace received a copy. I find Fr Kavanagh's reaction very gratifying and hope we can attain the standards I am endeavouring to establish.'[22]

This shows a change from the reverential tone of previous Supreme Knights' letters to McQuaid. Fr Kavanagh, later Auxiliary Bishop of Dublin, had been one of McQuaid's most trusted helpers in his governance of the diocese – Chairman of DICS, and member of the Vigilance Committee and Public Image Committee, among other responsibilities. This letter indicates he was on Grogan's side and supported the changes Grogan was advocating.

McQuaid eventually agreed in March 1967 to meet Grogan, Mgr MacMahon writing: 'The archbishop asks me to write to you concerning your request some time ago, on becoming Supreme Knight, to call on His Grace. His Grace is free tomorrow, Friday, 10th inst, at twelve noon, should it be convenient for you to call.'[23]

This was nearly seven months after Grogan's request for the meeting. The letter could not have reached Grogan before Friday morning. Was McQuaid expecting Grogan might not be free at such short notice or might not receive the letter in time? There is not any note in the archives about this meeting. Was there a connection between this sudden summons to Archbishop's House and Grogan's intention to participate in a *Seven Days* television programme about the Knights later that month? Grogan attended the episcopal consecration in 1968 of Bishop Joseph Carroll, another classmate from O'Connell School and the man whom McQuaid is believed to have wanted as his successor.[24]

The Knights, who in 1967 numbered some 1600 members in the Dublin area, about one quarter of their total membership, did not all go along with Grogan's *aggiornamento*. However, he continued his programme of reform and renewal throughout his three years in office. In his final message to the members, in 1969, he thanked those who had encouraged him by their co-operation, and added thanks also to 'you who, with sincerity and candour, have opposed some of my ideas or criticised my shortcomings'.[25]

An undated radio clip of Grogan shows how he found his relationships with the archbishop 'never easy, and, indeed, never happy'. He found him 'intractable' in private and 'certainly not malleable in his point of view'. Grogan believed McQuaid wanted those who were in some position to exercise or influence public opinion, like himself, 'to do so in entire deference and obedience to a very literal point of view which he took about Catholic doctrine'.[26]

There is very little correspondence in the diocesan archives relating to the Knights after Grogan. Luke Curran, the Newry solicitor who succeeded him as Supreme Knight, died in office in November 1971. The final entry in the archives is a letter from Curran, the month before his death, and two months before McQuaid's retiral, distressed and embarrassed that he had been told the archbishop was relying on a donation of £1000 towards the cost of a 'local film' dealing with the drug problem. Curran regretted that the Knights had not the funds to make such a donation as they had recently given help to the riot-stricken areas of Belfast and 'I could not go back to the brothers with another appeal'. He assured McQuaid that they would do their best to help him whenever they could, as they had, for example, in the case of the Communications Centre. McQuaid noted in reply that there had been some error, 'I was not given the assurance that the Knights would give £1000.'[27]

Vincent Gallagher says that Curran's deputy, and then successor, Paddy Hogan, a Galway businessman, was on very good terms with the archbishop and the members of the Order still recite a prayer for vocations composed by the archbishop at Hogan's request. Gallagher, who himself later served as Supreme Knight, adds that Dr McQuaid continued to visit the Knights at their headquarters in Ely Place, Dublin, as have his four successors. Paddy Hogan told me in April 1972 that, in fact, the Knights shared with the archbishop the cost of the drug film which was made by Radharc.[28]

A bleak outlook

Archbishop McQuaid, in October 1969, sent comments 'on our present situation' to Bishop Henry Murphy of Limerick, possibly in reply to an episcopal commission request for views. He believed there was great need to explain and insist upon the following of Jesus Christ in self-denial, particularly in temperance. The new affluence affords new opportunities for unchastity, excess in alcoholic drinking, unlawful expensiveness, neglect of debts, and in the case of those who have not ready money but must acquire it, larceny. The neglect of reasonably hard work, injustice towards employers are very common in the working class. Disregard for the person and interests of the workers is sadly evident in the attitude of many employers.

He lamented strikes that 'paralyse so many enterprises' and pointed to 'grave dangers' of urbanisation: '... for it displaces people, who, finding themselves in strange social conditions, tend to give up the practice of the faith'. He regretted family life was 'losing its sacredness' because family prayer was not being taught and insisted on by parents:

> ... Hearing the children their catechism, saying with them morning and night prayer till they could be trusted to pray themselves, reciting the family rosary are practices that are disappearing. The consequence is seen in the continuing failure to supervise the leisure and control the companions of the adolescents ...'

He believed young people were as generous as ever, 'it is in their nature', but emphasis on liturgical prayer was tending 'to eliminate the devotional practices that were the mainstay of the lives of our parents and grandparents'. He saw a serious obligation to instruct seminarians in 'the authentic doctrine of the church' and 'among the dogmas that most need to be explained and stressed is that of the teaching authority of the church, in both faith and morals, as the authentic documents of the church set forth that authority'.[29]

These are bleak sentiments. There is little sign of influence from the Council which was to renew the church, indeed the word 'Council' is not even mentioned. Was it that, having tried to move forward and engage with the world, John Charles McQuaid had now given up? There is evidence that between 1964 and 1968, especially after the Public Image Committee report, he tried to move with the times, in the spirit of Vatican II, and to engage with the changing world, but then he reverted, possibly because of shock at the response to *Humanae Vitae.*

Three letters on contraception

His initial handling of *Humanae Vitae* was balanced, but he was more outspoken in his final year, knowing he was retiring, when he issued three statements against contraception, one on 25 November 1970, the next with the Lenten Regulations on 17 February 1971 and then a pastoral letter on 22 March 1971. He stated in the first letter that in a diocese there is 'only one teaching authority' who

> under the Pope and in union with him, is competent, by virtue of his sacred office, to declare the authentic and objective moral law that is binding on all the faithful of his diocese, both priests and lay folk. That authority is the bishop.

He then 'formally' declared the 'doctrine of the objective moral law concerning the regulation of birth':

> ... every action which, either in anticipation of the marriage act or in accomplishment of that act, or in the development of the natural consequences of that act, proposes, either as an end or as a means, to make procreation impossible, is unlawful in itself. In other words, any such contraceptive act is wrong in itself. This is the constant teaching of the church.[30]

One reason for these letters was a Bill to legalise contraception in Ireland. It had been introduced by independent senators, Mary Robinson, John Horgan and Trevor West. In his March 1971 pastoral letter, condemning the proposed legislation, McQuaid asserted that if passed it would 'offend objective moral law' and 'would be, and would remain, a curse upon the country'.[31]

There were a lot of people in Ireland in those days who were still frightened by 'curses', but I remember my mother saying to me, up the stairs: 'He has gone too far. They will have to get rid of him.' John Horgan remembers it, particularly the reference to the 'curse' which would remain upon the country. He says even the other bishops were annoyed and believes that on this occasion McQuaid 'broke ranks and went right off down the middle of the field carrying the ball on his own'. It was his final, significant public uttering.

Fr Dermod McCarthy remembers the three statements but says they were not heeded, that McQuaid had 'become sidelined' by that time: '*Humanae Vitae* was quietly forgotten and anything that came after it was largely ignored … I clearly remember reading it and throwing it down in frustration and despair.' Historian Margaret MacCurtain believes that, at this stage, 'he was too old to grasp the significance of what he was issuing, that the subject of contraception had become so uncontainable that it was almost lip-service, that final pastoral …'[32]

Media after the Council

The Late Late Show, the RTÉ Saturday evening television chatshow, produced and presented by Gay Byrne, was believed by many to have a major influence on Irish society. It was an immediate success when introduced in summer 1962 and Byrne presented it until the late 1990s. Mgr Patrick Corish says some people date events as before and after the Council, 'more probably it was before and after *The Late Late Show*'. Mgr Corish believes it had an overall negative effect because 'Gaybo [Byrne] shot sacred cows and didn't have much to put in instead.' Gay Byrne still retains a friendly regard for Archbishop McQuaid who once wrote to thank him for defending him on *The Late Late Show*. Byrne's reply, marked 'personal' and on blue headed paper from his home in Howth, Co. Dublin, was 'McQuaidesque' in its brevity:[33]

> Your Grace.
> Thank you.
> Say one for me, please.
> Respectfully yours.
> Gay Byrne

Fr Roland Burke Savage marked John Charles McQuaid's episcopal silver jubilee in 1965 with a major profile in *Studies*.[34] Intended to answer critics, it raised old arguments and, by not answering them adequately, provoked renewed criticism, with *Herder Correspondence* dismissing it as an 'apologia' for McQuaid.[35] Fr Burke Savage persuaded McQuaid on the article, but McQuaid had misgivings and wrote: 'I really thought you had more sense. Imagine producing a pamphlet on my work up to summer 1965. Wait till I am dead (*The Times* editorial today shows you what you will be reading then).' Again: 'I cannot prevent you writing in your *Studies*. But a pamphlet horrifies me *adhuc vivus*. Be modest and give facts, not eulogy and think of all that remains to be done.' And again: 'But I shall not object to a merely factual study and for that you can have all the help you wish here'.[36] McQuaid told him he was not worried what he would write about him: '… it will be well-meant, I am sure and I shall endure it, like other aspects of the coming Jubilee.'[37]

On publication of the article, March 1966, McQuaid told Fr Burke Savage: 'I have now read for the first time your sketch in *Studies*. It has involved a very great deal of toil. For that and for the kindness with which you have treated me I am indeed grateful.'[38] However, this was a benign reaction to the article which he had himself seen and approved before publication, as Mgr Cecil Barrett, a man to whom he listened, had already expressed displeasure: 'Personally, I feel unable to accept the author's facile assessments … The section on the critics troubled me. However adequately critics would seem to be dealt with, I don't think one can really catch up on them.'[39]

It may have been McQuaid's more mature view some months later when, replying to Fr Burke Savage's accusations over the Mansion House meeting, he added: 'For your article [*Studies*]. I disliked the very idea of an article; I yielded to your importunity. I disliked the article: I allowed it through because of your very evident goodwill and very serious work. I dislike the article still.'[40] Fr Burke Savage had accused him of 'effectively disowning' him over the *Studies* article.[41] It was also the end of Burke Savage's biography idea. 'You will allow me to say that I do not want any biographies. After my death, there will be a deep silence.'[42]

Archbishop McQuaid and Louis McRedmond

McQuaid remained uneasy about journalistic coverage. He assured Papal Nuncio McGeough in 1968 he would do what he could in the future, 'as I have in the past, to diffuse knowledge of the Holy Father's statements as a counterbalance to the almost unlimited diffusion of the views of journalist theologians'.[43]

Louis McRedmond refers to liturgical directives which the archbishop issued to his clergy in 1969. The Press Office had issued a release, but not the full text. McRedmond obtained the directives and contrasted them with an earlier Roman document and 'put the two pieces side by side in the paper and asked what's going on, are we more Roman than the Romans?' He pointed to some directives which were not included in the press release. These included: temporary structures set in front of the high altar could not be used in any church or oratory, public or semi-public; Holy Communion was to be received kneeling; offertory processions in any church or oratory, public or semi-public, were not permitted; the practice of the faithful each placing a host in the ciborium on entering the church was not permitted; all musical instruments, other than the organ, were prohibited at church services.

In his *Irish Independent* report, headed 'Dublin priests distressed by directives', McRedmond referred to 'puzzlement that no explanation accompanied the directives. This would seem to be called for since most of the practices forbidden in Dublin are permitted generally or for special occasions in other Irish dioceses'. He said 'the whole tone' of the directives tended to 'jar with the corresponding instructions of the Holy See' in a 1967 document. One of these instructions was that other instruments, as well as the organ, could be permitted.[44]

Osmond Dowling, in a letter to the *Irish Independent* next day, took blame for any confusion, saying he selected those items which seemed to him to be 'of most interest to the general body of readers'. He listed nine other directives which he had not included and to which McRedmond did not refer. Dowling told McRedmond that the archbishop was 'greatly saddened'. McRedmond believes what upset McQuaid was the suggestion that he was not being fully obedient to Rome, that 'he was not implementing the Roman regulation ...' John Feeney also saw significance in these directives, as, to this point, McQuaid had loyally implemented the liturgical instructions of the Vatican, but 'now the decrees allowed a degree of spontaneity and difference from one area to another and John Charles, since it was not a direct instruction, fought against change'.[45]

Dowling noted to Mgr MacMahon, three weeks later, that letters in the *Irish Independent* on the liturgical reforms had now concluded. An editorial of that day had stated that all letters were published and the vast majority of them were critical, 10 against, four for, and three uncommitted. Dowling said that if over three weeks, only 17 of the 170,000 readers 'bothered to write on the subject it seems reasonable to draw certain conclusions'.[46]

In 1970, when *The Irish Times* asked Louis McRedmond, recently dismissed from editorship of the *Irish Independent*, to approach the archbishop with a view to doing a series of articles, he declined, not in the abrupt fashion of earlier years but, with his own reasons why a proper picture could not be provided. The letter was long and courteous:

> I fear that your editor, for all the good intentions that I am willing to allow him in this instance, would give you a quite impossible task. Unless you had access to my private archives you could not describe my episcopate. They will remain closed for long after my death. And they will contain many surprises for those who have already attempted to assess my years as Archbishop of Dublin.

McRedmond offered to show him the articles before publication but he felt that would also be a difficult exercise:

> I could not sanction the praise you might think it necessary to apportion. The blame you would find in me, I would as always allow to pass without comment. Both you – and your editor cannot fail to know that I have never yet answered when I was blamed or even reviled. I do not intend to change. All that side of one's life can be very safely left in the hands of God.[47]

This letter shows a measure of courtesy to *The Irish Times* and to McRedmond that McQuaid might not have shown some years earlier. There is a tolerance and sense of engagement with the journalistic reality, even if he still refuses to be interviewed. He would never have allowed 'good intentions' to *The Irish Times* in earlier years. However, he held out against giving interviews to the media. When T. P. Hardiman, newly appointed Director General of RTÉ, in 1968, had suggested an interview,

McQuaid was 'most unhappy' and quoted from the appropriate section of *The Imitation of Christ* on 'anonymity in the doing of the Almighty's work'.

Retiral and death

Margaret McMahon says Archbishop McQuaid, on his 75th birthday, got his secretary to bring her over 'and have a cup of tea and a piece of his birthday cake, a sponge cake, and he said, "You know, I officially retired today".'[49] The new regulation, brought in after the Council, was that all bishops must offer their resignation to the Pope at the age of 75, but he was not obliged to accept it. There were several Irish bishops older than McQuaid who had been allowed to stay on.

Fr Aidan Lehane says McQuaid always referred to his 'retiral' rather than 'retirement', indicating that his retirement was not voluntary. Fr Michael O'Carroll said McQuaid told him: 'I didn't retire. I was retired.'[50]

The archives show the sequence of events from McQuaid's resignation letter of July 1970, to 27 December 1971, the thirty-first anniversary of his consecration as archbishop, when Papal Nuncio Alibrandi called to his door to say the Pope had accepted his resignation, Fr Dermot Ryan, Professor at UCD, was his successor, and the announcement would be made the following week.

When Archbishop Diarmuid Martin of Dublin, then studying in Rome, was returning from Dublin in May 1970, Archbishop McQuaid gave him letters for Jean Cardinal Villot, Secretary of State and for Mgr Giovanni Benelli, number two in the Secretariat of State. He did not post them because there had been a postal strike in Italy. The Villot letter enclosed a greeting to the Pope on the 50th anniversary of his ordination as a priest, and a copy of McQuaid's pastoral letter on the subject. The covering letter to the Pope was a strong declaration that everything was all right in Dublin, the faith was safe and the priests and laity were loyal to the Pope, so he need not worry. The pastoral for the Pope's jubilee, published in full in *L'Osservatore Romano*, said those who knew Paul VI 'of one accord bear witness to the depth of divine faith that is the mainspring of his thought and word and action':

... Like the Son of God on earth, it has been his lot to be mis-represented, opposed, reviled and even hated. But is it not the promise of Jesus Christ, Our Lord, that the servant shall not be greater than his Master, and that men shall hate his faithful Apostles and disciples?[51]

The Benelli letter offered £10,000 for the reconstruction of the Papal Nunciature in Dublin: 'I shall see to it that the necessary funds will not be wanting. It is just one way of expressing to His Holiness my gratitude for a fatherly kindness that has never failed me.'[52] McQuaid sent the cheque to Alibrandi, but the money was eventually returned as it was decided not to rebuild the Nunciature but to relocate to nearby premises.[53]

Some have interpreted these letters as a tactic to prepare the Pope for the resignation offer two months later and this may have been so. Archbishop Martin has more recently been de-scribed as 'the conduit for the beleaguered McQuaid's unsuc-cessful countermove to prevent his removal which came 18 months later'.[54] This might be an exaggeration in fact, if not in intention. Archbishop Martin did not meet Cardinal Villot or Mgr Benelli on this occasion.

As Archbishop McQuaid approached his 75th birthday in July 1970, Osmond Dowling had media queries as to possible re-tirement and he told him he had been approached by all three Dublin daily papers: 'You will be aware of my response to all such enquiries: no comment. On being asked for my personal opinion, as I was, I replied that any such speculation on my part would be highly improper.' McQuaid noted: 'I fear I should re-gard any personal inquiry about my life as a grave intrusion, in very bad taste indeed. I have scrupulously refrained from mak-ing any inquiry into the personal life of journalists.'[55]

On return from vacation, Mgr Benelli, 8 August 1970, ac-knowledged a letter from McQuaid: 'Your Grace's accompany-ing letter addressed to Our Holy Father has already been handed to His Holiness. With pleasure I shall be delighted to see Your Grace when you come to Rome next month.' This letter to the Pope was clearly the offer of resignation.[56]

Newspapers had reported an audience of the previous year at which Pope Paul had given McQuaid a gold and ivory chalice

'in testimony of his fraternal benevolence and very grateful es-
teem'. Some interviewees mistakenly remembered this as the
Pope's way of saying the resignation had been accepted, but it
was eight months before the resignation letter. It may, however,
have been a hint from the Pope as to what was to come.[57]

Confirmation that McQuaid had submitted his resignation
came through an indiscretion by Fr Daniel O'Connell SJ, a
schoolfriend from Clongowes days, who was then recently retired as head of the Vatican Observatory, but still President of
the Pontifical Academy of Sciences. Irish Ambassador, Tommy
Commins, wrote to Hugh McCann, at the Department of
External Affairs, 11 November 1970:

> ... [Fr O'Connell] told me, in confidence, that Archbishop
> McQuaid, while here in Rome on a private visit in September
> last, did in fact offer his resignation to the Pope on the
> grounds of having reached the age of 75, and that it was de-
> clined. This presumably because of his obviously undimin-
> ished vigour, physical capacity and competence to continue
> the administration of the Archdiocese of Dublin for, maybe, a
> long time yet. Fr O'Connell, who has been a very close and
> intimate friend of his for the past 40 or so years at least, told
> me he had this information from the Archbishop himself.
> Archbishop McQuaid does not appear to have let anything of
> this be known to anyone else here and that is in character
> since as you know he is extremely reserved.[58]

Despite what McQuaid apparently told Fr O'Connell, the
resignation had been accepted and he had been told so. Nuncio
Alibrandi consulted him as to a suitable successor, writing, 18
December 1970, '*sub secreto pontificio*':

> Following our recent conversation I should be most grateful
> if Your Excellency would be so kind as to give me the names
> of three outstanding priests whom you would consider suit-
> able for the archdiocese. As this communication is under the
> Pontifical Secret, may I ask Your Excellency to return the let-
> ter with your reply.[59]

McQuaid did not return the original letter. Mgr Alibrandi
wrote again, 11 January 1971, '*sub secreto pontificio*':

The Prefect of the Sacred Congregation for Bishops, Cardinal Confalonieri directed me to inform Your Excellency that the Holy Father has praised the spirit of faithful submission and supernatural adherence to God's will, with which you received the communication concerning the acceptance of your retirement. His Holiness willingly accedes to your wishes in this matter and has ordered that the news should not be made public until after the next Synod of Bishops.[60]

Cardinal Villot told McQuaid the Pope had instructed 'you be allowed to continue to govern your archdiocese until after the forthcoming session of the Synod of Bishops'.[61]

McQuaid had already told Archbishop Finbar Ryan about the extra year being allowed to him, but might have led him to believe it could be longer, as Ryan wrote:

To borrow an image from Péguy, the months of 1970 have slipped through our hands like slippery eels, so that here we are again at Christmas and the beginning of an ominous new year. Need I say how much I wish and pray for your happiness at Christmas and for your fortitude in 1971 and after.[62]

He was possibly worried that the Pope's rapid acceptance of his resignation was a negative judgement on his work. Fr Lehane does not remember him ever being ill, so that was another reason for surprise that his resignation was accepted.

The 'retiral' features strongly in Fr Lehane's recollections and correspondence with McQuaid's friend, Dr J. Stafford Johnson. Fr Lehane says Stafford Johnson told him McQuaid was on edge every morning during these eighteen months, waiting for the 11 am post from Europe. 'It was like a sword of Damocles hanging over his head.' He didn't want to retire, but was prepared to accept it in obedience. He continued to visit Rockwell after retiral, where he was hosted by Fr Lehane, as President, and told him he had not attempted anything to influence the Pope's decision: 'I have done absolutely no juggling.'

Canon Paddy Battelle believes there was a 'push to get the resignation accepted' and a lot of people felt that change 'had to come, but a lot of us felt a bit sore at the way it did come about, in the sense that we felt that the man was toppled in the end, that there was clique in the diocese'. The name most often mentioned as part of the clique was Fr Dermot Ryan, Chairman of the Diocesan Council of Priests, and Professor of Eastern Languages at University College, Dublin. He was believed to be the popular choice for next archbishop. Mgr Ward agrees Fr Ryan was in favour of change and that priests also saw Fr James Kavanagh as a suitable successor. Fr Kavanagh was Professor of Social Science in UCD and, later, an Auxiliary Bishop of Dublin. One retired parish priest says there was a push and he was asked to become involved, but declined. Fr Dermod McCarthy also agrees about the push and believes McQuaid had 'suspicions' about it but never thought his resignation would be accepted. 'He couldn't believe it, that he who was archbishop of the most Catholic city in the world ...'

Mgr Tom Fehily agrees about the push and that Dermot Ryan was one of the people who spoke strongly about the need for a new archbishop. Mgr Fehily says they were close friends and former seminary classmates, but that Dermot Ryan 'was incapable of doing anything underhand; he would never have thought of doing that, but he felt that it was time for change'.

Bishop Donal Murray says people knew over those eighteen months that change was coming. He does not think there was 'a kind of agitation to get him to go. I would say they all knew it was coming', but there would have been 'a certain concern' about who might replace him. Bishop Murray remembers how, at short notice, McQuaid opened the new Mater Dei buildings in December 1971 and within a month he was gone: 'I think he had a hint.' He believes McQuaid expected to be left in office for another few years.

John Cooney's account supports Bishop Murray's view that the move was not against McQuaid, as all believed he was going anyway, but on who might be his successor. Cooney is critical of Dermot Ryan's role, saying he 'posed as a liberal in the Priests' Council to attract the support of the middle ground and the younger priests, and a campaign to promote him as McQuaid's successor had been led by priests such as Peter Lemass and Joe Dunn, who were well versed in communications'.[63] Fr Tony Gaughan was 'disgusted' when he learnt that the archbishop, after he tendered his resignation in 1970, 'had been undermined from within, in a disloyal and underhand fashion, by persons who were determined to ensure who would succeed him'.[64]

John Feeney reported that Mgr Alibrandi surveyed 'a wide number' of priests in early 1971 and 'a large majority' of the younger ones favoured a change of bishop, a view not shared by many of the city's parish priests. The majority of these younger priests favoured Dermot Ryan, with James Kavanagh in second place. They made it clear they did not want Bishop Carroll whom McQuaid saw as his 'heir-apparent'. Feeney says 'This must have been a bitter blow for Dr McQuaid and, in the end, the results of the survey were kept from him.'[65] It is difficult to see how the results might have been kept from him as versions were published in *The Irish Times* and *Evening Herald* with John Horgan (*The Irish Times*), hinting at names, not necessarily in order of choice, as Dermot Ryan, Bishop Donal Herlihy (of Ferns) and Archbishop Sean Gordon (Apostolic Delegate in Africa). Also, Fr Paul Tabet, in the Nunciature, noted Horgan's article to McQuaid expressing sorrow that 'such a delicate question should, once again, be a subject matter for the press'.[66]

Retiral

John Charles McQuaid behaved as normal from the Nuncio's visit to him on 27 December to mid-day, 4 January, when the Nuncio released the statement that the Pope had accepted the resignation and appointed Fr Dermot Ryan as archbishop. Bishop Murray tells how McQuaid himself announced it:

> ... he had a meeting with the vicars general at 11 o'clock. The meeting proceeded as normal, apparently. Then he said the Angelus and said: 'The new archbishop is waiting outside the door' ... That was extraordinary. But it was typical of him. He conducted the meeting as if nothing had happened ... He told Dermot Ryan to come to Archbishop's House at noon [by the postern gate, but Ryan did not know what a postern gate was, so had to ask the way!] ...

Mgr Ardle MacMahon concedes the archbishop was 'a little' disappointed, but 'never expressed his disappointment to me'. He says the archbishop would see his retirement in terms of obedience, 'that the Holy Father had accepted his resignation, that was the will of God for him. And he might not have spent that much time worrying about it … I felt he had a grip of things right up to the end.' Mgr MacMahon says he must have felt it coming 'because he did get an extension of a year or so'. This is the only confirmation in the interviews that he was given the extra year.

Fr Lehane remembers him saying: 'I will enthrone the new archbishop and then I will disappear completely. The next few years will be tough and perhaps I would not have been able for them. Perhaps I would let the church down.' He remembers, shortly afterwards, asking McQuaid for advice about something, and his reply was: 'There was a time when I could have helped you but remember I am in the vaults, in the vaults entirely.'

Fr Seán Fagan heard diocesan priests remarking that McQuaid resented the way the church was going: 'His time was over. He was very surprised and disappointed that his resignation was accepted in Rome … He gave the impression that he was so sure that his huge diocese was so well run that it was a model for others.' For Canon Battelle, 'it broke his heart' and Bishop Murray says 'it was a sad end, in a way'. Fr Lehane believes the Nuncio handled it badly because he informed him on the anniversary of his consecration.

Archbishop Finbar Ryan's great disappointment at his own retirement in 1966, through ill-health, and his return to Ireland in great gloom, would have affected McQuaid's foreboding of what might lie ahead of him. There was no other close friend to tell him what it would be like. Finbar Ryan wrote, 16 June 1966:

> You have been so long my friend and confidant that it is right you should be among the first to know of my resignation, accepted *propter aetatem et infirmitatem* [because of age and infirmity] … You, better than anyone, will understand my distress at seeming to fail the church at this crucial time here, and I can not free myself from the anxiety as to what may happen under a new regime … P.S. I die at noon Roman time on Saturday, 18th.[67]

Finbar Ryan hated retirement, 'I die'. He believed he could not be done without and feared those whom he did not favour would take over and ruin all he had done. McQuaid would have reflected on this as his own time approached.

In August 1966, Finbar Ryan, now back in Cork, wrote:

> ... I find it difficult to adjust myself to such a circum-scribed and seemingly aimless life. My departure from Port of Spain was unspectacular but not without a feeling that personally, I had failed God, and that deservedly I was being taken from the people of my love. This I have said to nobody but yourself!

To the end

Dermot Ryan was ordained Archbishop by the Pope, in Rome, and came back to Dublin for his installation, in the Pro-Cathedral, 27 February 1972. Archbishop McQuaid adminis-tered the diocese until then. Canon Battelle, then a curate in the Pro-Cathedral, remembers him that day: 'When I was helping him with his vestments, he said: "Father, Father, they didn't want me".' He says McQuaid was 'very hurt' and that 'he put on his coat and walked out the back door' and didn't stay for the reception. Another priest who was present, seeing retirement as 'the worst thing that ever happened' to McQuaid, confirms this story. Vincent Gallagher continued to visit him in retirement. Fr Joe Dunn never met him in retirement and wrote:

> ... it's something I still feel badly about. He moved quite sud-denly from a position of great power and activity to one where he was powerless, unemployed, and semi-ostracised. Rightly or wrongly, some seemed to suggest that to call at Killiney, where John Charles lived, might be taken as a symbol of oppo-sition to the new regime. So I decided to wait a little.

One close friend says McQuaid felt the transition from a very busy pastoral schedule of work to the experience of the inactivity of retirement, 'but he had inner reserves which supported him'. He agrees McQuaid felt lonely in retirement because he was a quiet person by style and he never socialised as such.

In that year he was thinking a lot of death, as shown in his re-marks to Mgr Fehily about his fear of dying and facing judge-ment. Mgr Fehily visited him weekly during retirement. He talks of the integrity of the man, he was lonely, he never complained about anything, he never said, 'nobody visits me' or that, he never said, 'how is the new archbishop getting on', or 'how are things in the diocese' ... He never mentioned anything to do with the diocese.

Mgr Fehily says Archbishop McQuaid, after retirement, only came to ceremonies if he was invited, and 'he rarely was invited. I would imagine he was very hurt ... I don't think Dermot [Ryan] visited him much, if at all...' Fr Tom Butler talks of his great faith. He had a few letters from him after retirement, and 'I don't think he was ever disillusioned ... possibly, I would say, he was a bit disappointed'.

The *Sunday Press*, in March/April 1973, ran a series of articles on the Dublin archdiocese, with one criticising the state of the diocesan finances and suggesting Archbishop McQuaid had been reckless in overburdening the diocese with debt to build new churches and other developments. There was not any suggestion of dishonesty.[70] Fr Lehane says McQuaid was 'deeply upset'. He was not to read the next two articles for, on the following Saturday morning, 7 April, he had a heart attack, was taken to hospital and died. Fr Lehane says Dr Stafford Johnson attributed 'the unexpected heart attack' to the articles, 'because they were not contradicted'. He says Stafford Johnson told him in a letter in 1978: 'It was the trigger that brought about his death and no doubt God had his own designs on this. I have his own annotated copy [of the articles]'.

John Cooney learnt from Fr Michael O'Carroll that McQuaid was 'so distressed' that he went to Mgr Cecil Barrett and said 'it is putting my whole period in office in question'.[71] Mgr Barrett advised him to do nothing because the media would seize upon any statement.

Cardinal Connell believes Archbishop McQuaid was treated 'very unfairly'. He himself was 'deeply hurt' at the way 'a great man had been attacked':

But, I was a friend of Dermot Ryan and I could speak openly to him. I said to him, not attacking him, because I was quite convinced that he hadn't inspired them [the articles], I said: 'Your predecessor always did the dignified thing. There was only one dignified thing to do on this occasion, and that was to die, and the Lord permitted him to do so.

And this was Archbishop John Charles McQuaid's final answer to his critics.

CHAPTER EIGHT

Summary

This book has discussed the enigma of Archbishop John Charles McQuaid and the seemingly contradictory aspects of his personality and management style, especially within the context of the Second Vatican Council and its aftermath. He was an outstanding, efficient, and even revolutionary administrator and a forceful, strategic thinker, looking ahead and recognising sooner than others the importance of oncoming issues. At the same time, he was kind and charitable, always solicitous for the individual person and their welfare, especially those who were under-privileged, poor, sick or in trouble of any sort.

In religious matters, he was predominantly solicitous for that vast majority of his people to whom he referred as the 'simple faithful'. He was their 'shepherd' and his utmost concern was that they would not be confused or disturbed in their religious faith and practice and that he would pass on to them and their children the 'deposit of faith', untarnished and intact.

The public man could be quite off-putting, with a concentration on ceremonial and formality, and servants administering to him, all which he saw as proper respect for the office of bishop, but which was viewed by some as arrogance and vanity. He sought control of every situation he was involved in, was authoritarian and often severe in his management style, placing high importance on unquestioning obedience and strong discipline. Despite this, he had a charismatic and enduring impact upon those who knew him closely, or even only met him closely once or twice. He is still 'The Archbishop' to many and Mgr Stephen Greene referred repeatedly to his 'pontificate', even when I drew his attention to this unusual description.

There is fresh evidence here that certitude, even in impossible situations, was a strong influence in John Charles McQuaid's life. First, he had certitude that, as archbishop, appointed by the

Pope, he was the sole teaching authority on faith and morals in his diocese. He did not want to be seen to change, especially under pressure, because that could imply that his previous teaching was now in error and his credibility as a teacher could be undermined.

He tried to extend this certitude into private conversations, preparing topics even before informal and social meetings and then insisting on taking the lead and having the last word. His encyclopedic memory and grasp of detail helped him in this. Friends did not remember him ever admitting to be wrong or not to know something.

Certitude in his spiritual life and relationship with God was the most private and probably the most important to him. His spiritual director told him in 1930 of his recurring tendency to seek an impossible certitude of the senses in his spiritual life and an impossible knowledge of his progress. His director rebuked him for falling back into this tendency even when it was pointed out to him as false. He probably never lost this anxiety for spiritual certitude.

Evaluating the Second Vatican Council
and Archbishop McQuaid's response to it
It is still difficult, even after more than forty years, to assess the success or failure of the Second Vatican Council. There is still confusion, as it meant different things to different people. Patience is still needed, the Catholic Church is an old institution and has always moved slowly, and history alone will show if the Council was a success or a failure.

To the liberals, the Council was at first seen as a success with many changes in discipline and the interpretation of doctrine, bringing in a certain element of democracy and openness, emphasising that the entire People of God, the laity with Pope, bishops and priests, are the *church*. There seemed to be a drawing-back after *Humanae Vitae* in 1968 which, some would say, continued through the long pontificate of John Paul II (1979-2005). Archbishop McQuaid believed that his own response to the Council, in total obedience to the Pope, was a success in that the changes were made in Dublin and, as he told the Pope, the faithful remained 'in very greatest proportion, true to the faith, and the practice of the faith'. Some other bishops in the world could not claim this outcome.

While he was a model of diligence in the way he attended every session, every meeting of the Council, and studied and responded to the documentation in fine detail, at first he, along with the other Irish bishops, may not have appreciated how important it would be. Minutes of hierarchy meetings fail to mention it during the months leading to the opening in October 1962 apart from asking people to pray for its success. There was no explanation of what the Council might be about, nor invitation to contribute views and ideas about it.

At the start of the Council, Archbishop McQuaid played down extreme hopes, warning what 'not to expect' and reiterating his views on Protestants having to turn 'towards the only truth'. However, he was encouraging at the same time in saying he would accept its decrees and loyally execute its commands.

He was alarmed at the liberal trends in the First Session but then set about trying, unsuccessfully, to arrange lectures for the Irish bishops so they would be better informed next session. He continued the diocesan outreach lectures for adults, which now began to deal with Council topics among others, but the older priests were not always supportive. There has been widespread and justified praise for his initiative in the Radharc film unit, which anticipated the importance of television. He continued to allow his priests to work in it, and did not try to influence the subjects covered, not even the programmes on the dissatisfaction of nuns after the Council.

In 1963, he established a Centre of Religious Studies and Information to inform non-Catholics and help lay people understand theology, but warned Fr Burke Savage, its director, that he did not want it 'confused as an ecumenical gesture' or another measure of *aggiornamento* 'wrung from the archbishop' by the criticism of journalists and others. He established the Public Image Committee to find from his priests what really was the image of the church (and himself) in Dublin and what changes were needed. People would have been encouraged if they had known about this but he insisted on absolute secrecy. He then set up the Diocesan Press Office and won praise for it, but then kept too firm a control, deciding all policy, allowing little latitude to Osmond Dowling and often, to Dowling's embarrassment and humiliation, not keeping him properly informed. He gave tacit approval to the Marist Fathers' new altar in Milltown and said nothing but sent priests to have a look at it before reorganising their own parish churches.

He gave his 'No Change' address about Council changes not 'worrying the tranquillity of your Christian lives' but assured, again, that all of its decrees and subsequent directives would be fully obeyed. He accepted the changes but would, as far as possible, dictate the pace of their implementation in his diocese, despite criticism. He did not say that he was acting strictly in accord with Cardinal Lercaro's secret instruction.

He went along with Fr Burke Savage's idea for the Mansion House ecumenical meeting, and was again praised, but he did not react to the situation when the seating arrangements went chaotic and he could easily have invited Archbishop Simms up to the empty chair on the platform. The Diocesan Council of Priests was another early initiative but he weakened it by appointing all of the initial members and emphasising they were merely a consultative body.

He met Archbishops Ramsey and Simms at Archbishop's House, but resisted and then grudgingly consented, when Osmond Dowling advised on the photocall. Mater Dei Institute was another example of his foresight and his desire to have religion teachers and laity better informed in theology, but some saw it as an attempt to reinforce his own bastion of orthodoxy at Clonliffe College against his concern about Maynooth's orthodoxy. However, he allowed liberal theologians to lecture in Mater Dei without apparent interference.

When the hierarchy decided Catholics could attend weddings, baptisms and funerals of non-Catholic friends, he told Bishop Herlihy of Ferns: 'It will take a lot of explaining to my people.' Again, on Cardinal Bea's draft directory on ecumenism, he pleaded Dublin's 'special circumstances', saying ecumenism in Dublin was 'a gravely delicate process' and that Bea was not the Archbishop of Dublin, where the situation needs 'very delicate handling'.

Gestures were offered courteously, especially to the Church of Ireland, but he seems eventually to have given up the effort to adapt and change, possibly over disappointment at the widescale criticism and rejection of *Humanae Vitae*. He welcomed the encyclical with enthusiasm, and, unlike other bishops, such as Cornelius Lucey in Cork and Patrick O'Boyle in Washington DC, he handled the fall-out better, was discreet with those whom he knew were not in full support, and avoided public rebukes or sackings of his priests.

The end of the Trinity College ban went against his wishes but he accepted it while complaining when the bishops decided he must appoint a chaplain at Trinity, 'the first occasion on which the Episcopal Conference will have forced a measure on an individual bishop'. Finally, he obediently offered his resignation on his 75th birthday, and accepted the decision of the Pope, but pleaded and got an extension of one year.

In summary, John Charles McQuaid identified the Council as a key issue for the church and his diocese, and seems to have managed efficiently his diocese's responses to it. However, he lacked power over the development and presentation of the Council and, as the media became more pervasive, he could not control those who spoke and wrote about it, even in Dublin. He would like to have been able to control the change himself and he attempted vigorously to gain control over religious broadcasting on Telefís Éireann but, after a lengthy battle, he failed.

Ireland changed in the 1960s in many ways – political, economic, social, educational, cultural, religious. It was a decade of rapid change in the whole world. The Vatican Council was just one factor in that dramatic process of change. Some would say one of the more important factors was communication, especially television and the *Late Late Show*. In the 1960s there was a new appetite for debate amongst the Catholic laity, even if their knowledge of theology was often slight, and they fed upon the dramatic media presentation of the Council and the views of speculative theologians. Their interest was shown in packed attendances at Milltown Park public lectures and the small, but interested Group that Archbishop McQuaid described as Fr Flannery's 'salon in my diocese'. It was witnessed in the enthusiastic readership for paperback theology.

Archbishop McQuaid could react to, but no longer control the developments that were taking place around him, and was slow to realise, for example, that his traditional methods of censorship were no longer effective in the face of television and a more well-informed and questioning press. His communication was traditionally one-way, allowing little or no room for discussion – he was the old-fashioned teacher. He took advice but he alone had the full picture of his position on any issue.

His first pre-occupation was always for the 'simple faithful' not to be upset. He didn't mind who attacked him as long as 'the faith' didn't suffer. He knew there was not unanimity about change among clergy or laity, and being the man at the top, it was difficult for him to drive a middle course. This would be another reason why he moved slowly on the changes and why he had fewer negative and traditionalist reactions than in some other parts of the world. He could probably have given a better lead and could have been more positive about the opportunities offered by the Council, instead of being on the defensive. The Public Image Committee regretted he was not giving 'positive leadership that would give them [priests and faithful] pride and confidence in their church'.

He dominated life in Dublin over his long episcopacy, his style of rule was autocratic, politicians were influenced by, and even submissive to, his wishes. That was true, but not surprising as he was probably the last in a long line of dominant Irish bishops who saw all to do with education, politics and everything that might affect their people, as their rightful domain. He realised that, by tradition, he had been given great power and influence and he endeavoured to use it. He seems a throwback to that era of 'political' bishops, but a much milder version when compared, for example, with Cardinal Cullen of Dublin (1852-78).

One could overestimate his influence on priests or laity in the 1960s when a lot of change seemed to have passed him by. There remained the apparent contradictions between the public man and the private man, an intriguing, sensitive and even endearing man, but quite vulnerable and deeply hurt by his 'enemies'. Also, the element of fear which he is supposed to have generated among priests and laity can be exaggerated. The priests were intelligent men, doing their daily work, but the 'fear' of the archbishop became such a legend, especially among those who did not know him, that it never lifted.

The laity had a long tradition of deference to and reverence for their bishops and priests, and much has been made of their reaction to *Humanae Vitae* and McQuaid's final three letters against the proposed legislation to legalise contraception. It was not the first time that Irish people had disagreed with their bishops, especially when it included a matter of politics. Also, there were other smaller incidents which showed that the Dublin people, despite the aura of their archbishop, did not hesitate to make up their own mind when they disagreed with him and felt he had gone beyond his domain. Politicians, knowing the influence that bishops traditionally had with so many people, were only being prudent when they considered episcopal attitudes in advance of legislation.

The changes in the 1960s in Ireland brought a new generation of younger politicians. Ambassador Tommy Commins' reports to the government from the Vatican, criticising the Irish bishops for their 'supine and reserved' attitude at the Council and their lack of leadership or impact, may have been a factor in these politicians realising that bishops were no longer the force they had been. They certainly acted that way when, without consulting the bishops, they proposed the Dublin university merger in 1967. McQuaid welcomed the idea of the merger because he believed it would finally be the end of Protestant Trinity College. But as the debate went on, he was shocked when he heard the NUI Senate had accepted that the Trinity ban would go and he had been 'left in the dark'.

It is difficult to make a judgement on the Council, and even on John Charles McQuaid's handling of it, as success or failure have different meanings for liberals and conservatives, with many other positions in between. The Council issue, destined from the start to become permanently embedded in history, remains a cyclical one, so that its long-term effects could not have been predicted at the time, nor even now, more than 40 years on. McQuaid, in protecting the 'simple faithful', seems to have succeeded in the short-term, although there were signs of fall in Mass attendance and other church devotions. He also kept his team of priests intact, with very few resignations until after he had retired. He went ahead in his own way, no matter who criticised him, and made all of the changes that were decreed.

Notes

CHAPTER ONE

1. McQuaid, J. C., *Wellsprings of the Faith*, Dublin, Clonmore and Reynolds, 1956, 209

2. Sheehy, D. C., 'Archbishop McQuaid: Legend into History', *Doctrine & Life* 53:2, February 2003,105

3. McQuaid, J. C., *Wellsprings of the Faith*, Dublin, Clonmore and Reynolds, 1956, 124-5

4. Dublin Diocesan Archives (DDA): AB8/B/XXVI/e/78 – Committee on the Public Image of the Church

5. Feeney, J., *John Charles McQuaid – The Man and the Mask*, Cork, Mercier Press, 1974, 1

6. DDA: AB8/B/XXVI/c/25 – Diocesan Press Office, April-May 1965

7. Coogan, T. P., *Ireland Since the Rising*, London, Pall Mall Press, 1966

8. DDA:AB8/B/XX – Dublin Institute of Catholic Sociology

9. DDA: AB8/B/XVI/03 - Vatican

10. DDA: AB8/A/11 – Blackrock College, 1925-40 (Fahey letter not in file)

11. Cooney, J., *John Charles McQuaid, Ruler of Catholic Ireland*, Dublin: The O'Brien Press, 1999, 13

12. DDA: AB8/B/XXVI/e/78 – Committee on the Public Image of the Church

13. DDA: AB8/B/XXVI/d/66 – Communications, Print Media, Studies

14. DDA: P9 – Burke Savage papers

15. McGarry, P., 'A Man for All Seasons', interview with Otto Herschen, *The Irish Times*, 13/1/2004

16. Cooney, J., *John Charles McQuaid, Ruler of Catholic Ireland*, Dublin, The O'Brien Press, 1999, 35

17. DDA: AB8/B/XV/c/5 – Foreign bishops: Central/South America and West Indies

18. RTÉ 1 Television, 'John Charles McQuaid – What the Papers Say', presented by John Bowman, 9/4/1998 and 16/4/1998

19. DDA: AB8/B/XXVI/d/59 – Communications, Print Media, *The Irish Times*

20. DDA: P9 - Burke Savage papers

21. Ibid.

22. DDA: AB8/B/XXVI/e/78 – Committee on the Public Image of the Church

23. Cooney, J., *John Charles McQuaid, Ruler of Catholic Ireland*, Dublin, The O'Brien Press, 1999, 432

24. DDA: AB8/B/XXVI/a/3 – Communications, Television, RTÉ 1960-71

25. Feeney,J., *John Charles McQuaid – The Man and the Mask*, Cork, Mercier Press,1974, 1

26. RTÉ 1 Television, 'John Charles McQuaid – What the Papers Say', presented by John Bowman, 9/4/1998

27. University College Dublin (UCD) archives: Prof John Whyte papers – notes from McQuaid interview, 14/8/1969

28. Kirby, P., 'Memories of John Charles: An Archbishop at Home', *Doctrine & Life*, 40:6, July-August 1990, 317

29. DDA: AB8/B/XVII/09 – Papal Nuncios, Sensi

30. DDA: AB8/B/XXVI/e/78 – Committee on the Public Image of the Church

31. DDA: P9 - Burke Savage papers

32. DDA: AB8/B/XXVI/e/78 – Committee on the Public Image of the Church

33. Ibid.

34. Sheehy, D. C., 'Archbishop McQuaid: Legend into History', *Doctrine & Life* 53:2, February 2003,108

35. DDA: AB8/B/XXVI/e/78 – Committee on the Public Image of the Church

36. Dunn, J., *No Tigers in Africa!*, Dublin, The Columba Press, 1986, 25

37. University College Dublin (UCD) archives: Prof John Whyte papers – notes from McQuaid interview, 14/8/1969

38. Burke Savage, R., 'The Church in Dublin: 1940-65', *Studies* 54: Winter 1965, 320

39. Ibid., 322

40. DDA: AB8/B/XV/a/1 – Irish Bishops, Box 2: G-W

41. University College Dublin (UCD): Prof John Whyte papers – notes from McQuaid interview, 14/8/1969

42. DDA: AB8/B/XXVI/c/28 – Diocesan Press Office, October 1965

43. 'George Knowall', *The Nationalist & Leinster Times*, 15/10/1965

44. DDA: P9 – Burke Savage papers

45. Ibid.

46. Barrett, C., 'John Charles McQuaid – The Man They Knew', *Mission Outlook*, June 1973, 7

47. DDA: AB8/B/XXVI/c/34 – Diocesan Press Office, March-April 1966

48. Cooney, J., *John Charles McQuaid, Ruler of Catholic Ireland*, Dublin, The O'Brien Press, 1999, 59

49. Lennon, P, *The Manchester Guardian*, January 8-11, 1964, reference in DDA: P9 – Burke Savage papers

50. DDA: AB8/B/XXVI/d/73 – Communications, Print Media, Various Journals

51. DDA: AB8/B/XXVI/e/78 – Committee on the Public Image of the Church

52. DDA: P9 – Burke Savage papers

53. Ibid.

54. UCD: Prof John Whyte papers – notes from McQuaid interview, 14/8/1969

55. DDA: AB8/B/XXVI/c/26 – Diocesan Press Office, June-July 1965

56. DDA: AB8/B/XXVI/d/68 – Communications, Print Media, *Herder Correspondence*

57. DDA: AB8/B/XXVI/c/26 – Diocesan Press Office, June-July 1965

58. DDA: AB8/B/XXVI/d/68 – Communications – Print Media, *Herder Correspondence*

59. DDA: AB8/B/XXXX/c/33 – Diocesan Press Office, 1966-67, Jan-Feb 1966, with copy of *Daily Telegraph* supplement, 21/1/1966: 'DUBLIN – City of Skies and self-styled moral guardians'

60. DDA: AB8/B/XVI/03 – Vatican

61. DDA: P9 – Burke Savage papers

62. Carty, F.X., 'Archbishop of Dublin Experiencing Storm', Copley News Service, USA, 1969 (syndicated to West Coast papers)

63. 'Gay Byrne Defends Archbishop', *Sunday Press*, 19/1/1969

64. Feeney, J., 'The End of an Era? A Profile of Most Rev. J. C. McQuaid', *This Week*, 1:41, 31/7/1970, 30-4

65. Feeney, J., *John Charles McQuaid – The Man and the Mask*, Cork, Mercier Press, 1974, 79

66. Ibid., 88

67. DDA: AB8/B/XXVI/d/59 – Communications, Print Media, *The Irish Times*

68. DDA: AB8/B/XV/a/1 – Irish Bishops, Box 2:G-W

69. Heenan, J.C., *Not the Whole Truth – an Autobiography*, London, Hodder & Stoughton, 1971, 242-3

70. Cooney, J., *John Charles McQuaid, Ruler of Catholic Ireland*, Dublin, The O'Brien Press, 1999, 161

71. DDA: AB8/B/XV/a/1 – Irish Bishops, Box 1:A-F

72 UCD: Prof John Whyte papers – notes from McQuaid interview, 14/8/1969

CHAPTER TWO

1. Kaiser, R., *Inside the Council*, London, Burns & Oates, 1963, 18

2. Küng, H., *The Council and Re-Union*, London, Sheed and Ward, 1961

3. McNamara, K., *Christian Unity*, Maynooth, The Furrow Trust, 1962, viii

4. Hurley, M., 'Vatican Council and the Ecumenical Situation Today', *Irish Ecclesiastical Record* (1962) 98:35

5. McCarthy, C., 'Looking Back at the Sixties', *Reality* 33i: 12, 2-4, December 1969, 2

6. Fuller, L., *Irish Catholicism Since 1950*, Dublin, Gill & Macmillan, 2002, 30

7. RTÉ Radio 1, 'Interview with Archbishop Diarmuid Martin', *Tonight with Vincent Browne*, 23/12/2003

8. Küng, H., *My Struggle for Freedom: Memoirs*, London, Continuum, 2003

9. Garvin, T., *Preventing the Future: Why Was Ireland Poor for So Long?*, Dublin, Gill & Macmillan, 2004, 56

10. Cooney, J., *John Charles McQuaid, Ruler of Catholic Ireland*, Dublin, The O'Brien Press, 1999, 17

11. Ibid., 271

12. Rynne, X., *The Second Session*, New York, Farrer Strauss, 1964, 111

13. De la Bedoyere, M., *The Layman in the Church*, London, Burns & Oates, 1954, 6

14. National Archives of Ireland (NAI): 14/86/1 – 24/184, P.R. 17/60 – Holy See

15. DDA: AB8/VC/XLV/1 – Preparation for Council

16. *Acta et Documenta Oecumenico, Vaticano II Apparando; Series 1 (Antepraeparatoria); Vol 2: Consilia et Vota Episcoporum ac Praelatorum, Pars II Europa*, Vatican, Typos Polyglottis Vaticanis, 1970

17. Ibid., 77-80

18. DDA: AB8/B/XVII/08 – Papal Nuncios, Riberi (11/4/1960)

19. DDA: AB8/B/XV/b/05 – Hierarchy Minutes, 1962-65

20. DDA: AB8/B/XV/a/1 – Irish Bishops, Box 2: G-W

21. Fuller, L., *Irish Catholicism Since 1950*, Dublin, Gill & Macmillan, 2002, 108

22. Olden, M., 'Irish Catholicism: Reflections', (Review of Fuller, 2002), *The Furrow*, 54:4, April 2003, 243

23. Hurley, M (ed), *Christian Unity: An Ecumenical Second Spring?*, Dublin, Veritas, 1998, 341-7

24. DDA: P9 – Burke Savage papers

25. DDA: Knights of St Columbanus

26. DDA: AB8/B/XXVI/c/30 – Diocesan Press Office 1965: Director's addresses and correspondence

27. DDA: AB8/B/XX – Dublin Institute of Catholic Sociology, 9/6/1967

28. DDA: AB8/B/XV/a/1 – Irish Bishops, Box 2: G-W, 28/2/1961 and 1/3/1961

29. Feeney, J., *John Charles McQuaid – The Man and The Mask*, Cork, Mercier Press, 1974, 41

30. Tobin, F., *The Best of Decades – Ireland in the 1960s*, Dublin, Gill & Macmillan, 1984, 44

31. McMahon, D., 'John Charles McQuaid: Archbishop of Dublin, 1940-72', in J. Kelly & Daire Keogh (eds): *History of the Catholic Diocese of Dublin*, Dublin, Four Courts Press, 2000, 371

32. DDA: AB8/B/XXVI/a/4 – Communications: Television Training for Dublin Priests (Radharc)

33. Ibid.

34. Ibid., 25/1/1960

35. Dunn, J (1986): *No Tigers in Africa!*, Dublin, The Columba Press, 1986; Dunn J., *No Lions in the Hierarchy*, Dublin, The Columba Press,

1994; Dunn, J., *No Vipers in the Vatican*, Dublin, The Columba Press, 1996

36. DDA: AB8/B/XXVI/a/4 – Communications: Television Training for Dublin Priests (Radharc),

37. Ibid.

38. Ibid.

39. Ibid.

40. Ibid.

41. Peter Dunn, Director of The Radharc Trust, in communication to author, April 2007

42. Dunn, J: *No Tigers in Africa*, Dublin, The Columba Press, 1986, 132.

CHAPTER THREE

1. DDA: AB8/VC/XLV/2 – Preparation for First Session

2. DDA: AB8/VC/XLV/6 – Meetings with UK Hierarchies

3. DDA: AB8/VC/XLV/12 – Lecturers for Second Session

4. DDA: AB8/B/XV/b/05 – Hierarchy Minutes, 1962-65

5. NAI: S.24/184, Shelf 2/305/4 – Vatican Council Second and Third Session, 1963-64

6. Ibid.

7. Ibid.

8. Ibid.

9. DDA: AB8/B/XXVI/c/25 – Diocesan Press Office, April-May 1965

10. Wood, K., 'A Bishop's Candid Memories of Vatican II (Archbishop Thomas Morris)', *Catholic World News* 1997 (from 1992 article in Catholic World Report). http://www.cwnews.com/Browse/1997/01/4091/htm (30/8/02).

11. DDA: P9 – Burke Savage papers

12. DDA: AB8/VC/XLV/7 – Appointments First Session

13. DDA: AB8/VC/XLV/3 – Correspondence during First Session

14. *Acta Synodalia Sacrosancti Concilii Oecumenici Vaticano II, Vol. I: Periodus Primus, Pars I, Sessio Publica I, Congregationes Generales I-IX*, Vatican. Typis Polyglottis Vaticanis. 1970, 414

15. Rynne, X., *Letters from Vatican City*, London, Faber & Faber, 1963, 108

16. *Acta Synodalia Sacrosancti Concilii Oecumenici Vaticano II, Vol. I: Periodus Primus, Pars II, Congregationes Generales X-XVIII*, Vatican, Typis Polyglottis Vaticanis, 1970, 44

17. DDA: AB8/VC/XLV/3 – Correspondence during First Session

18. Rynne, X., *Letters from Vatican City*, London, Faber & Faber, 1963, 118

19. *Acta Synodalia Sacrosancti Concilii Oecumenici Vaticano II, Vol. II: Periodus Secundus, Pars V, Congregationes Generales LXV-LXXIII*, Vatican, Typis Polyglottis Vaticanis, 1970, 566

20. DDA: AB8/VC/XLV/9b – Archbishop's speeches, Third and Fourth Sessions

21. Ibid.
22. Cooney, J., *John Charles McQuaid, Ruler of Catholic Ireland*, Dublin, The O'Brien Press, 1999, 366
23. DDA: P9 – Burke Savage papers
24. *Acta Synodalia Sacrosancti Concilii Oecumenici Vaticano II, Vol. II: Periodus Secundus, Pars IV, Congregationes Generales LIX-LXIV*, Vatican, Typis Polyglottis Vaticanis, 1972, 260
25. DDA: AB8/VC/XLV/23a – Interventions etc Third and Fourth Sessions
26. DDA: AB8/VC/XLV/9b – Archbishop's speeches, Third and Fourth Sessions
27. DDA: AB8/B/XXVI/e/78 – Committee on the Public Image of the Church
28. McQuaid, J.C., *The Sacred Liturgy* (Pastoral Letter), 20/2/1964
29. DDA: AB8/B/XVII/09 – Papal Nuncios, Sensi
30. DDA: AB8/B/XXVI/e/78 – Committee on the Public Image of the Church
31. DDA: Legion of Mary
32. McRedmond, L (ed), *Modern Irish Lives*, Dublin, Gill & Macmillan, 1996, 89
33. Hartigan, M., 'The Religious Life of the Catholic Laity in Dublin, 1920-40', in James Kelly & Daire Keogh (eds): *History of the Catholic Diocese of Dublin*, Dublin: Four Courts Press, 2000, 338
34. Cooney, J., *John Charles McQuaid, Ruler of Catholic Ireland*, Dublin, The O'Brien Press, 1999, 109
35. Ibid., 118
36. O'Carroll, M., 'Inspired Educator and Ecumenist of Sorts', *Studies* (1998), 87: No 308, 371
37. DDA: Legion of Mary
38. Ibid.
39. Ibid.
40. Ibid.
41. McRedmond, L., 'Dialogue in the Church, 1: The Journalist', *The Furrow* (1964), 15:1, 6
42. McRedmond, L., *The Council Reconsidered*, Dublin, Gill & Son (Logos Books), 1966, 7
43. Horgan, J., 'Remembering How Once We Were' (Review of L. Fuller book), *Doctrine & Life* (2003), 53:4, 24
44. DDA: AB8/B/XXVI/e/78 – Committee on the Public Image of the Church
45. DDA: AB8/B/XXVI/a/4 – Communications: Television Training for Dublin Priests (Radharc)
46. McNicholl, A., 'Looking Back on the Council', *Irish Ecclesiastical Record* (1966), 105:153
47. DDA: AB8/B/XXVI/c/27 – Diocesan Press Office, August-September 1965

48. Ibid.
49. Ibid.
50. Fuller, L., *Irish Catholicism since 1950*, Dublin, Gill & Macmillan, 2002, 234-5
51. DDA: AB8/B/XV/a/3 – Other Churches
52. Butler, C., 'The Council Phase 1', *The Tablet* (London), 31/8/1963
53. DDA: AB8/B/XV/b/05 – Hierarchy Minutes 1962-65
54. DDA: AB8/B/XV/b/07 – Hierarchy Minutes 1968-69

CHAPTER FOUR

1. Kirby, P., 'Memories of John Charles: An Archbishop at Home', *Doctrine & Life*, 40:6, July-August 1990, 319
2. DDA: AB8/VC/XLV/3 – Correspondence during First Session
3. Ibid.
4. McQuaid, J.C., *Second Vatican Council – First Session* (pastoral letter), 7/3/1963
5. DDA: AB8/B/XXVI/e/78 – Committee on the Public Image of the Church
6. DDA: AB8/VC/XLV/14a – General Correspondence at Second Session
7. DDA: AB8/B/XXVI/e/78 – Committee on the Public Image of the Church
8. DDA: AB8/B/XV/a/1 – Irish Bishops, Box 1: A-F
9. Philbin, W., *The Meaning of the Vatican Council* (pastoral letter), Belfast, February 1966
10. Cooney, J., *John Charles McQuaid, Ruler of Catholic Ireland*, Dublin, The O'Brien Press, 1999, 398
11. Power, B.,' How Christian are the Students?', *Reality* 33:6–10, June to October 1969
12. Novak, M., *The Open Church – Vatican II Act II,* London, Darton, Longman & Todd, 1964
13. Masterson, P., 'An Open Church?', *The Irish Ecclesiastical Record*, 102: December 1964, 417-32
14. DDA: AB8/VC/XLV/23 – General Correspondence during Third Session
15. *A New Catechism – Catholic Faith for Adults*, London, Burns & Oates, 1967 (The 'Dutch Catechism')
16. DDA: AB8/B/XVII/10 – Papal Nuncios, McGeough
17. DDA: AB8/B/XXVI/e/78 – Committee on the Public Image of the Church
18. Masterson, P., 'Paperback Theology', *The Furrow*, Supplement 1, Spring, 1967, 1-4
19. DDA: AB8/B/XXVI/e/78 – Committee on the Public Image of the Church
20. Ibid.
21. Ibid.

22. DDA: AB8/B/XV/a/1 – Irish Bishops, Box 1: A-F

23. DDA: AB8/B/XXVI/e/78 – Committee on the Public Image of the Church

24. Dowling, O.G., 'Poetry Ban' (letter to editor), *The Irish Times*, 26/2/1965

25. DDA: AB8/B/XXVI/c/23 – Establishment of Diocesan Press Office, March 1965

26. Ibid.

27. Ibid.

28. Ibid.

29. Ibid.

30. DDA: AB8/B/XXVI/c/25 – Diocesan Press Office, April-May 1965

31. DDA: AB8/B/XXVI/c/29 – Diocesan Press Office, November-December 1965

32. DDA: AB8/B/XXVI/c/28 – Diocesan Press Office, October 1965

33. DDA: AB8/B/XXVI/c/38 – Diocesan Press Office, January-June 1967

34. Ibid.

35. DDA: AB8/B/XXVI/c/27 – Diocesan Press Office, August-September 1965

36. DDA: AB8/B/XXVI/c/37 – Diocesan Press Office, 1966: 'Mansion House affair'

37. DDA: AB8/B/XXVI/c/38 – Diocesan Press Office, January-June 1967

38. O'Mahony, T.P., 'Scheme to Pay Priests', *Evening Press*, 6/4/1968

39. DDA: AB8/B/XXVI/c/43 – Diocesan Press Office, April-June 1968

40. DDA: AB8/B/XXVI/e/78 – Committee on the Public Image of the Church

41. DDA: AB8/B/XXVI/c/43 – Diocesan Press Office, April-June 1968

42. DDA: AB8/B/XXVI/c/47 – Diocesan Press Office, July-December 1969

43. Freeney, P., 'Dublin Priests Meet', *Doctrine & Life*, 19:10, October 1969, 568-71

44. DDA: AB8/B/XVII/11 – Papal Nuncios, Alibrandi

45. DDA: AB8/B/XXVI/c/50 – Diocesan Press Office, July-December 1970

46. DDA: AB8/B/XXVI/c/55 – Diocesan Press Office, World Communications Day, 1967-70

47. McQuaid, J.C., 'Sermon for World Communications Day, 1967, at Clonliffe College', Dublin Diocesan Bulletin, 1967:1

48. DDA: AB8/B/XXVI/d/59 – Communications, Print Media, *The Irish Times*

49. DDA: AB8/B/XXVI/c/38 – Diocesan Press Office, January-June 1967

50. Cooney, J., *John Charles McQuaid, Ruler of Catholic Ireland*, Dublin, The O'Brien Press, 1999, 382

51. *Irish Catholic Directory*, Dublin, James Duffy & Co., 1968, 726

52. DDA: AB8/B/XXVI/c/36 - Diocesan Press Office, October-December 1966

53. DDA: AB8/B/XV/b/04 - Hierarchy Minutes, 1958-61

54. DDA: AB8/B/XXVI/a/10 - Hierarchy Television Committee, 1960-63

55. DDA: AB8/B/XXVI/a/9 - Appointment of Priest Advisor to RTE, 1961-63

56. DDA: AB8/B/XXVI/a/3 - Communications, Television, RTE 1960-71

57. DDA: AB8/B/XXVI/a/11 - Hierarchy Television Committee, 1964-67

58. Ibid.

59. Ibid.

60. Ibid.

61. Ibid.

62. DDA: AB8/B/XXVI/a/3 - Communications, Television, RTE 1960-71

62. Ibid.

CHAPTER FIVE

1. DDA: AB8/B/XXVI/c/33 - Diocesan Press Office, January-February 1966

2. Fisher, D., 'The Post-Vatican Council Church in Ireland', *The Kerryman*, 20/5/1967

3. DDA: AB8/VC/XLV/37 - General Correspondence, Fourth Session

4. Ibid.

5. Ibid.

6. Wood, K., 'A Bishop's Candid Memories of Vatican II (Archbishop Thomas Morris)', *Catholic World News* 1997 (from 1992 article in Catholic World Report). http://www.cwnews.com/Browse/1997/01/4091/htm (30/8/02)

7. Cooney, J., *John Charles McQuaid, Ruler of Catholic Ireland*, Dublin, The O'Brien Press, 1999, 371

8. McDermott, P., 'Plus ça Change', (letter to editor), *The Irish Times*, 16/12/1965

9. DDA: AB8/B/XVII/09 - Papal Nuncios, Sensi

10. DDA: AB8/B/XV/a/3 - Other Churches

11. McQuaid, J. C., *Our Faith* (pastoral letter), 1968

12. DDA: AB8/B/XV/b/06 - Hierarchy Minutes 1966-67

13. Ibid.

14. DDA: AB8/B/XXVI/d/59 - Communications, Print Media, *The Irish Times*

15. DDA: AB8/B/XV/a/1 - Irish Bishops, Box 1: A-F

16. Ibid.

17. Ibid.

18. Ibid.
19. DDA: AB8/B/XXVI/c/25 – Diocesan Press Office, April-May 1965
20. Burke Savage, R., 'The Church in Dublin: 1940-65', *Studies*, 54: Winter 1965, 327
21. DDA: AB8/B/XXVI/c/27 – Diocesan Press Office, August-September 1965
22. DDA: AB8/B/XXVI/c/51 – Diocesan Press Office, January-June 1971
23. DDA: AB8/B/XV/a/1 – Irish Bishops, Box 2: G-W
24. Ibid.
25. DDA: AB8/B/XV/a/1 – Irish Bishops, Box 1: A-F
26. DDA: AB8/B/XX – Dublin Institute of Catholic Sociology
27. DDA: AB8/B/XXVI/c/50 – Diocesan Press Office, July-December 1970
28. DDA: AB8/B/XV/c/5 – Foreign bishops: Central/South America and West Indies
29. DDA: AB8/B/XXVI/c/25 – Diocesan Press Office, April-May 1965
30. DDA: AB8/B/XV/b/05 – Hierarchy Minutes 1962-65
31. Carty, F.X., 'The Irish People and Their Priests 7: Is Preaching Dead?', *Irish Press*, 20/11/1967(Fr Dunn interviewed)
32. DDA: AB8/B/XV/b/06 – Hierarchy Minutes 1966-67
33. DDA: AB8/B/XXVI/c/46 – Diocesan Press Office, January-June 1969
34. DDA: AB8/B/XXVI/c/48 – Diocesan Press Office, January-March 1970
35. RTÉ 1 Television, 'Interview with Bishop W. Walsh', *Would You Believe?*, Aine Ní Chiaráin, November 2002
36. NAI: S.24/184, Shelf 2/305/4 – Vatican Council, Second and Third Sessions, 1963-64
37. DDA: AB8/VC/XLV/14a –General Correspondence at Second Session
38. Ibid.
39. DDA: A B8/B/XV/a/1 – Irish Bishops, Box 1: A-F
40. DDA: AB8/B/XV/b/08 – Hierarchy Minutes, 1970
41 DDA: AB8/B/XXVI/c/36 – Diocesan Press Office, October-December, 1966
42. DDA: AB8/B/XV/b/07 – Hierarchy Minutes 1968-69
43. 'Priest to Meet Parish Critics', Evening Press, 4/11/1968
44. DDA: AB8/B/XXVI/c/44 – Diocesan Press Office, July-December 1968
45. DDA: AB8/B/XV/a/1 – Irish Bishops, Box 1: A-F
46. Ibid.
47. DDA: AB8/B/XXVI/e/78 – Committee on the Public Image of the Church
48. Carty, F.X., 'The Irish People and Their Priests 7: Is Preaching Dead?', *Irish Press*, 20/11/1967

49. DDA: AB8/B/XV/b/07 – Hierarchy Minutes 1968-69

CHAPTER SIX

1. Tobin, F., *The Best of Decades – Ireland in the 1960s*, Dublin, Gill & Macmillan, 1984, 189
2. *The Irish Times*, 22/1/1966
3. *The Irish Catholic Directory*, Dublin: James Duffy & Co, 1967, 715
4. DDA: AB8/B/XXVI/d/66 – Communications, Print Media, *Studies*
5. DDA: P9 – Burke Savage papers
6. Ibid.
7. Ibid.
8. Ibid.
9. Ibid.
10. Ibid.
11. Ibid.
12. Ibid.
13. DDA: AB8/B/XXVI/c/33 – Diocesan Press Office, January-February 1966
14. Cooney, J., *John Charles McQuaid, Ruler of Catholic Ireland*, Dublin, The O'Brien Press, 1999, 375
15. DDA: AB8/B/XXVI/d/66 – Communications, Print Media, *Studies*
16. DDA: P9 – Burke Savage papers
17. DDA: AB8/B/XX – Dublin Institute of Catholic Sociology
18. Hamell, P.J., 'The Ecumenical Movement', in K. McNamara (ed): *Christian Unity*, Maynooth: The Furrow Trust, 1962, 19-20
19. NAI: 14/86/1 – 24/184, Shelf 2/305/4 – Vatican Council, Second and Third Sessions, 1963-64
20. DDA: AB8/B/XXVI/e/79 – Communications, Centre of Religious Studies and Information
21. *The Irish Times*, 16/2/1965
22. 'Curial Mentality in Dublin Archdiocese', *Herder Correspondence*, July 1965, 195-99
23. DDA: AB8/B/XV/a/1 – Irish Bishops, Box 2: G-W
24. DDA: AB8/B/XXVI/e/78 – Committee on the Public Image of the Church
25. DDA: AB8/B/XV/b/06 – Hierarchy Minutes 1966-67
26. Ibid.
27. UCD: Prof John Whyte papers – notes from McQuaid interview, 14/8/1969
28. DDA: AB8/B/XV/a/3 – Other Churches
29. Ibid.
30. Ibid.
31. DDA: AB8/B/XXVI/c/38 – Diocesan Press Office, January-June 1967
32. *Irish Catholic Directory*, Dublin, James Duffy & Co, 1969, 727

33. 'Church Unity' (editorial), *The Irish Times*, 15/1/1968
34. Quoted in *Irish Catholic Directory*, Dublin: James Duffy & Co, 1969, 727
35. DDA: AB8/B/XXVI/c/43 – Diocesan Press Office, April-June 1968
36. DDA: AB8/B/XV/a/3 – Other Churches
37. Ibid.
38. DDA: AB8/B/XV/a/1 – Irish Bishops, Box 1: A-F
39. DDA: AB8/B/XV/a/3 – Other Churches
40. McQuaid, J.C., Pastoral letter, January 1971
41. 'All Out of Step', (editorial), *Sunday Independent*, 24/1/1971
42. DDA: AB8/B/XXVI/c/40 – Diocesan Press Office, 1967: Trinity Ban
43. UCD: Prof. John Whyte papers – notes from McQuaid interview, 14/8/1969
44. DDA: AB8/B/XV/b/04 – Hierarchy Minutes, 1958-61
45. DDA: AB8/B/XXVI/e/78 – Committee on the Public Image of the Church
46. Cremin, P.F., 'Church Unity Week in Trinity College – Some Impressions and Comments', *Irish Ecclesiastical Record*, 103: June 1965, 357-60
47. DDA: AB8/B/XXXII/A/1-11 – UCD, President Michael Tierney, 1959-64; President J. J. Hogan, 1964-72, UCD/TCD merger
48. 'Lent I', (editorial), *The Irish Times*, 6/2/1967 and 'Lent II', (editorial), *The Irish Times*, 13/2/1967
49. 'Attacks on Archbishop of Dublin' (editorial), *Sunday Independent*, 12/2/1967
50. DDA: AB8/B/XXVI/c/40 – Trinity Ban
51. DDA: AB8/B/XXXII/A/1-11 – UCD, President Michael Tierney, 1959-64; President J. J. Hogan, 1964-72, UCD/TCD merger
52. DDA: AB8/B/XV/a/1 – Irish Bishops, Box 2: G-W
53. Ibid.
54. DDA: AB8/B/XV/b/08 – Hierarchy Minutes, 1970
55. Ibid.

CHAPTER SEVEN

1. Daly, G., 'Catholic Fundamentalism', in A. Hanley & D. Smith (eds): *Quench Not the Spirit*, Dublin, The Columba Press, 2005, 131
2. Kaiser, R. B., *The Encyclical That Never Was*, London, Sheed & Ward, 1987
3. *Irish Catholic Directory*, Dublin, James Duffy & Co, 1969, 752
4. *The Irish Times*, 26/11/2001
5. DDA: AB8/B/XV/a/1 – Irish Bishops, Box 1: A-F
6. *Irish Catholic Directory*, Dublin, James Duffy & Co, 1969, 751-3
7. DDA: AB8/B/XVI/03 - Vatican
8. Ibid.
9. Irish Episcopal Conference (1968): 'Statement on *Humanae Vitae*', *Irish*

Ecclesiastical Record 110:183-4

10. DDA: AB8/B/XV/b/10 – Hierarchy Correspondence

11. Keogh, Dermot, *Twentieth-Century Ireland – Nation and State*, Dublin, Gill & Macmillan, 1994, 267

12. Fuller, L., *Irish Catholicism since 1950*, Dublin, Gill & Macmillan, 2002, 235

13. FitzGerald, G., *All in a Life – An Autobiography*, Dublin, Gill & Macmillan, 1991, 84

14. DDA: AB8/B/XV/c/4 – North American Bishops

15. DDA: AB8/B/XV/a/1 – Irish Bishops, Box 1: A-F

16. DDA: AB8/B/XXVI/c/44 – Diocesan Press Office, July-December 1968

17. 'Crisis in the Church', (editorial), *Irish Independent*, 8/8/1968

18. DDA: AB8/B/XV/a/1 – Irish Bishops, Box 1: A-F

19. Horgan, J., 'Catholic Magazine of Controversy Folds' (*Herder Correspondence*), *The Irish Times*, 28/5/1970

20. DDA: Knights of St Columbanus

21. Ibid.

22. Ibid.

23. Ibid.

24. DDA: AB8/B/XV/a/1 – Irish Bishops, Box 2: G-W

25. Ibid.

26. RTÉ Radio 1: *'What If? The Appointment of John Charles McQuaid as Archbishop of Dublin'*, presented by Diarmuid Ferriter, 11/1/2004

27. DDA: Knights of St Columbanus

28. Carty, F. X., 'The Truth about the Knights', *Sunday Independent*, 23/4/72

29. DDA: AB8/B/XV/a/1 – Irish Bishops, Box 2: G-W

30. McQuaid, J.C., Statement, 25/11/1970

31. McQuaid, J.C., *Contraception and Conscience* (pastoral letter), 22/3/1971

32. RTÉ Radio 1: *'What If? The Appointment of John Charles McQuaid as Archbishop of Dublin'*, presented by Diarmuid Ferriter, 11/1/2004

33. DDA: AB8/B/XXVI/a/3 – Communications, Television, RTÉ, 1960-71

34. Burke Savage, R., 'The Church in Dublin: 1940-65', *Studies*, 54: Winter 1965, 297-336 (published March 1966)

35. 'Burke Savage, Roland, SJ: 'The Church in Ireland: 1940-65' (a review), *Herder Correspondence*, April 1966

36. DDA: P9 – Burke Savage papers

37. Ibid.

38. Ibid.

39. DDA: AB8/B/XXVI/d/66 – Communications, Print Media, *Studies*

40. DDA: P9 – Burke Savage papers

41. Ibid.

42. Ibid.

43. DDA: AB8/B/XVII/10 – Papal Nuncios, McGeough
44. McRedmond, L., 'Dublin Priests Distressed by Directives', *Irish Independent*, 2/4/1969
45. Feeney, J., *John Charles McQuaid – The Man and the Mask*, Cork, Mercier Press, 1974, 69
46. DDA: AB8/B/XXVI/c/46: - Diocesan Press Office, January-June 1969
47. DDA: AB8/B/XXVI/d/59 – Communications, Print Media, *The Irish Times*
48. Horgan, J., *Broadcasting and Public Life – RTÉ News and Current Affairs, 1926-1997*, Dublin, Four Courts Press, 2004, 62
49. RTÉ 1 Television, *'John Charles McQuaid – What the Papers Say'*, presented by J.Bowman, second programme, 16/4/1998
50. Ibid.
51. DDA: AB8/B/XVI/03 - Vatican
52. Ibid.
53. Ibid.
54. *The Phoenix*, 15/8/2003
55. DDA: AB8/B/XXVI/c/50 – Diocesan Press Office, July-December 1970
56. DDA: AB8/B/XVI/03 – Vatican
57. Ibid.
58. NAI: 98/2/06 – Holy See Private Papers, 1967-70
59. DDA: AB8/B/XVII/11 – Papal Nuncios, Alibrandi
60. Ibid.
61. Ibid.
62. DDA: AB8/B/XV/c/5 – Foreign Bishops: Central/South America and West Indies
63. Cooney, J., *John Charles McQuaid, Ruler of Catholic Ireland*, Dublin, The O'Brien Press, 1999, 426-7
64. Gaughan, J. A., *At the Coalface – Recollections of a City and Country Priest 1950-2000*, Dublin, The Columba Press, 2000, 101
65. Feeney, J. (1974:74): *John Charles McQuaid – The Man and the Mask*, Cork, Mercier Press, 1974, 74
66. DDA: AB8/B/XVII/11 – Papal Nuncios, Alibrandi
67. DDA: AB8/B/XV/c/5 – Foreign Bishops: Central/South America and West Indies
68. Ibid.
69. Dunn, J., *No Tigers in Africa!*, Dublin, The Columba Press, 1986, 35
70. Kelly, J., 'Church and its Money', *Sunday Press*, 1/4/1973
71. Cooney, J., *John Charles McQuaid, Ruler of Catholic Ireland*, Dublin, The O'Brien Press, 1999, 431

Index